Pea Soup for the Packer Heart

A Tribute to the World's Greatest Fans & Team!

Steve Rose

with Kathi Rose

Winners Success Network Publishing
Neenah, WI

Pea Soup for the Packer Heart
A Tribute to the World's Greatest Fans & Team!
by Steve Rose with Kathi Rose

First Edition, first printing
Copyright 2010 by Steve & Kathi Rose

ISBN: 0-9666819-9-1

For more information or to inquire about author engagements and/or contributor signings go to:

www.peasouppackerbook.com

Winners Success Network Publishing
Box 404
Neenah, WI 54957-0404

Publisher: Steve Rose
Editor: Kathi Rose

Book idea, stories and contributor relations, Steve Rose
Editing and rewriting, Kathi Rose
Executive assistance to Steve Rose by Mike Utech
Book layout by Loralee Olson-Arcand, Word Services Unlimited
Cover design concept by Laura Taylor, To-the-Point Marketing
Cover photo by Debbie Daanen Photography, Appleton, WI
Cover photo thanks to and permission from Tim & Cindy McGray
Other assistance provided by Dale Rose
Printed in the USA by Seaway Printing, Green Bay, WI
Photograph permission has been granted wherever necessary

Table of Contents

Dedication

To Dale, my brother and friend. When we stand side by side I look down on you, but in my heart and soul I look up to you with respect, adoration and gratitude for the way you have been such a great help and role model for me. Thanks for listening to and caring about my dreams and for helping to make them a reality, like this book.

Love,
Steve

Dale & Steve Rose

Acknowledgments

We would like to thank the many people who have helped to make this Packer tribute a reality. We salute the greatest fans in all of sports who have submitted their stories; the media who has been gracious and cooperative during this project; the Green Bay Packer players, past and present, who've been so great to work with. A big tip of the hat goes to Jeff Blumb and to those in the Packer organization who've been incredibly helpful, too. We appreciate each and every one of you.

Steve & Kathi Rose

Foreword

I am from Green Bay. It's my hometown. When people ask, "Where did you grow up?" I answer with pride. It is perhaps the most unique professional sports town in the world. In what is an improbable story of survival, the Packers have remained solvent by every means possible, through wars and depressions, league expansion, free agency and a massive renovation of Lambeau Field.

This franchise doesn't have an individual owner. The fans own the team. It is the only team in major pro sports in this country that has that distinction. It's understandable, then, that the pride Packer fans feel is something to which no other pro sports fan can relate. That's why the Packer fan is different from others in sports. That's why the atmosphere at Lambeau is so special. That's why the tailgating is more than just a get together. It's more ritual really. The emotions are stronger among Packer fans. The passion is deeper.

Being a Packers fan is carried from generation to generation. It's about tradition, win or lose. It's more than a game, or a team. It's family. It matters.

The Packer fan has so much invested, time, emotion and money in some cases. And in clothing Packers fans will buy anything with the "G" logo or the name "Packers" on it. They love this team. They love the story.

Steve Rose has captured the wonderful stories associated with the *Packers in Pea Soup for the Packer Heart*. Some of the stories are told by the common fan, other stories are recounted by very familiar names. Blended together, they bring, through their words, a portion of the Packers story.

I have been lucky enough to have a front row seat. My dad began working for the team in 1971. I was 10. I have watched games from the stands. I have stood on the sideline as a ball boy. I now watch from the press box, broadcasting games to national audiences. The Packers have been a part of our family's life, as they have yours.

It just takes one moment to experience something that will last a lifetime. Here are some of those moments.

By Kevin Harlan

Introduction

The conception of this book began with a simple idea that had been brewing in Steve's mind for some time. He wanted to share twenty of his favorite warm and fuzzy untold Packer stories, and asked a few of his friends if they'd like to share theirs, as well.

What started as a small collection quickly grew as word spread about the project. More and more green-and-gold fans began to offer their own stories, which, until now, were only being shared around America's kitchen tables, over a beer at the local sports bar, or at a tailgate party in Lambeau Field's parking lot. These are stories you won't hear during football on FOX, NBC, CBS or ESPN, and you won't read them in Sports Illustrated or even your local newspaper's sports section, but they're just as worthwhile.

This book is for you, the fans of this special community-owned franchise. I believe you are now holding one of the most unique collections of fan, player and media stories ever written. I hope you find it as pleasurable to read them as Steve and I did collecting and writing them.

So, sit back and enjoy a delicious helping of Pea Soup. We hope it will warm your Packer heart.

By Kathi Rose

1 Kabeer & Bob on Tour

There's little-to-no ego inside the business offices at 1265 Lombardi Avenue in Green Bay, WI, home of the greatest professional sports franchise in the world, the Green Bay Packers. What seems to matter most is that the job gets done, whatever that may look like. The main goal, understandably, is to provide the Packer coaching staff with the tools they need to win the Super Bowl, which the team has done three times now.

In 2000, the Green Bay Packers drafted Kabeer Gbaja Biamila, an outgoing, talented young man from the University San Diego State. He quickly became known in the land of green-and-gold and around the NFL as simply "KGB." Born in Los Angeles, the big city boy found himself in small town USA, content and grateful for the opportunity to fulfill his dream of becoming a professional football player.

After one of his first practices with the team, KGB wandered over to the offices where management conducted business. Acting as if he owned the place, Kabeer ambled his 6'4" well-sculpted body down a hall until he finally found someone.

"Hi, I'm Kabeer," he waved from the doorframe of a big office to the man sitting behind his desk.

"Hi, I'm Bob," greeted the smiling, energetic gentleman.

Bob approached the rookie who went on to explain just why he was visiting the executive quarters.

"I was just drafted and I pretty much know what happens as a player, but I'd like to know more about what you guys do here in the office." Bob instantly abandoned his immediate plans and proposed an idea.

"Kabeer, how about I give you a tour and show you just what it is we do around here?"

"That'd be great. Thanks."

Further down the hallway, Bob introduced the rookie to Andrew Brandt and a few other Packer administrative personnel. As the tour continued, KGB had many questions, and Bob had equally as many answers. Finally, they arrived at a huge and immensely impressive room. Kabeer was completely captivated now as Bob explained to him where they were, and proceeded to give him a history lesson as to why the Packers are so unique, not only in the NFL, but in the entire world of professional sports.

"Kabeer, this is where the Packer Executive Board meets to make many significant and key decisions. You see, we're owned by the fans, which is just one of the many reasons Green Bay and this team are so special."

Kabeer expressed his appreciation for the time Bob had spent with him, but he had one more question for Bob before hitting the weight room.

"By the way, Bob, what do you do here?"

"Well, when I am not giving tours, I'm the President!"

I suspect there are very few professional sports owners or executives, making their millions of dollars each year, who would take time from their busy day to do what Bob did. But both Green Bay and Bob Harlan are unique.

Harlan retired in 2008 and was succeeded by Mark Murphy. Bob, in addition to having one of the most successful runs of any NFL President in the business, is one of the kindest and most generous of individuals I've ever had the pleasure to meet. The pace of the Pack is the pace of the leader, and for many years the Packers were led by one of the finest leaders in the business.

Bob has been nothing but incredibly gracious to me with his time, whether it was to sit down with me and talk, or to answer my questions by phone. Speaking of which, it might interest you to know that Bob always answered his own phone, no secretaries or gate keepers. Bob Harlan epitomizes what's right in sports. He's been one reason why the Green Bay Packers remain so special. Today, Mark Murphy has taken the reins and, like Bob, understands that this is "white-collar" business in a "blue-collar" world.

Whether you know a Packer player personally, or you simply are a fan, you'll truly enjoy these stories. If you have had the terrible "misfortune" of never experiencing this particular sports phenomenon, let me assure you that you're in the right place to learn all about it.

Let me also put out a warning: If you begin this book as a fan of any other team, there's more than a distinct possibility that you could find yourself, by the end of this book, wearing the green-and-gold.

And if you're ever in Green Bay and would like a tour of 1265

Lombardi ask for Bob. If he's in, there's a strong possibility he'll actually give you one!

By Steve Rose with help from Bob Harlan

ೞ ಐ

2 The Packer Taxi Cap

Perry Kidder is one of the nicest men I know. He's also one of the biggest Packers fans around. Perry's learned that when he travels abroad there are a few key things to pack: tickets, a passport, Travelers Checks and a supply of Packer caps.

Circa 1993. The Green Bay TV executive was in Hong Kong entertaining a group of his stateside clients. Perry, his wife Donna, and their friends landed in Hong Kong via Tokyo. The business trip was also providing an opportunity for a bit of sightseeing, as well.

"We'd been told to make sure we went to Stanley Square. Once we had checked in at the Hilton downtown, we hailed a taxi, and in no time were on our way," Kidder said.

It didn't take the Oriental driver long to notice the logo on Perry's hat, which was of the green-and-gold Wisconsin variety. Kidder believes the Packers logo may be one of the top ten brands in the world. I doubt he'd get much of an argument over that contention. Still, Perry was a bit surprised when the driver began chatting in broken English about the Green Bay Packers! Now, there may have been a slight language barrier, but "Packer-ese" is a language all its own.

"I watch Green Bay Packers. They very good," he prattled somewhat nervously. "I like Brett Favre. I think team great! I think they win Super Bowl soon," remarked the somewhat edgy driver who came off as a bit unpleasant.

Kidder could only smile in amazement. Their driver was cold, direct and overbearing, but he did share one bond with his fare from stateside.

"Here we were, half-way around the world, and we're having a conversation with this guy who was a Communist sympathizer. In one breath he would talk radical politics and then switch back to talking about the Packers," Perry remembers.

One thing never changed, however, during the entire ride.

"Somehow, he kept one eye on the road, and the other on my hat," recalls Perry. "And I gotta tell ya, this guy knew his stuff. He was an incredibly knowledgeable Packer fan. And clearly, I could tell, he wanted my hat!"

"I want that hat!" The words finally came from the intimidating voice of the driver.

"No friend. I can't give you this hat," Perry told him calmly, but firmly.

"I need Packer hat," the driver demanded one more time.

Again, Perry refused. The ride took another awkward fifteen minutes. Finally the tourists arrived at Stanley Square. Kidder was already calculating his next move.

"He pulled up to where we wanted to get out. I could see that he's fuming a bit. He really wanted my hat, and it was apparent he was ready to cut a deal. So as we got out, I asked, 'How much?'" Kidder smiled to himself as he recreated the scene for me.

Perry already knew what was coming next.

"Gimme hat!" the driver yelled, knowing he had been "had" by Perry.

Kidder just smiled and handed the ornery driver his Packer hat for the one-hour fair, which should have been a very costly one under ordinary circumstances. The driver squealed his tires as he left Perry and the group at the curb. Perry chuckled as he told his friends his secret.

"I learned a valuable lesson when I was being taxied around Caracas, Venezuela," he smiled as they walked. "I have three more back in the room!"

By Steve Rose with memories from Perry Kidder

CB EO

3 My Friend Mac

In the early to mid 1970s ('73-'76), I was an on-air personality at WYNE in Appleton, WI. Each year, on April Fool's Day, we had members of the Green Bay Packers do our radio shows. During those years I got to meet many of the guys from those '70's teams and became friends with a few of them, including Chester Marcol, Noel Jenke, Rich McGeorge, and Scott Hunter.

My greatest experience, by far, was being befriended by the great running back MacArthur Lane. One small but satisfying memory was when I gave Mac some disco and soul albums that the record companies would send us. We only played 45 rpm records on the station, so he and his wife were the happy recipients of some of the great music that they loved.

Mac was a wonderful, personable, friendly man. I believe that one of the main reasons for the great success of John Brockington's rushing records back then was that Lane was his fullback and Mac would do the blocking to open up the holes for John. After the 1974 season Mac went to the Kansas City Chiefs, and in 1976 I went to Tampa (the city, not the Bucs).

Even after leaving the Packers, Mac and I still kept in touch by mail and phone calls. During the fall of 1976 my parents and aunt and uncle came to visit me in Tampa. When the Chiefs came to play the Buccaneers, Lane arranged for tickets to the game for my dad, uncle and me. After the game he came out to spend a few minutes with us. He was incredibly gracious to me and my family. He became part of the family, calling my dad "Dad" and my uncle "Uncle Dave." We were all quite captured by his down-to-earth friendliness. He posed for a picture with my father at the stadium, which has become one of my dad's most prized possessions. He had it enlarged, framed and placed next to the cash register at the tavern he owned, Hec's Bar in Ashland, WI.

Until the day he died, Dad would show customers that picture and talk about what a great guy "his friend" MacArthur Lane was. My father, Vernon "Hec" Bennett passed away in 1994. Our family still considers

Vernon "Hec" Bennett with MacArthur Lane

this picture one of our most special mementoes.

I don't doubt that this is just one of many stories that could be told about an unselfish man who spent a short time in Green Bay, but who left the community better for his time there. By the way, the people at Hec's in Ashland think he's pretty special, too.

By Charlie Bennett

CR SO

4 Anna's Game is Favre from Over

Anna Walentowski is one amazing girl with an even more amazing story of perseverance, odds-busting and love. Football players in Green Bay have the reputation of being the tough guys, but they don't hold a candle to this tyke!

Anna was born in 1998, pre-term at about 34.5 weeks to her parents Jeff and Jennifer. In early infancy, Anna underwent an MRI which indicated a brain abnormality. Then, at age four, Anna was diagnosed with a growth hormone deficiency and began receiving daily shots of human growth hormone while continuing challenging physical therapy. At that same time, she began early childhood special education, but Anna's condition steadily declined.

Occasionally Anna seemed to have difficulty with swallowing. During one frightening episode she began to choke while eating her meal at a restaurant. She recovered, but only after the Heimlich maneuver was administered. Eventually she began to complain during mealtimes about not feeling well, or not wanting to eat at all. In October of 2003, she had a bad bout of stomach flu. It took a few weeks to fully recover. Even after her recovery, she continued to look unusually pale, and the family began to worry. Clearly, something was not right.

By Christmas of 2003, Anna's challenges dramatically escalated. She began to lose weight, a serious concern given she was already quite small and underweight for her age. Things did not improve. By age six, she weighed less than 38 pounds and eventually she dropped down to 33 pounds. Anna's apparent and seemingly progressive deterioration caused a doctor at Children's to recommend her to Make-A-Wish. Her case was reviewed, Jackie VerVoort (Make-A-Wish representative) met with the family, and the Foundation worked swiftly to grant Anna's wish to meet Brett Favre and the Green Bay Packers.

Anna's particular wish was one with which the family was comfortable, particularly since their primary concern was one of logistics. Due to Anna's medically fragile condition, and the "out of nowhere" breathing problems, they didn't want to travel too far from known care providers. Anna had enjoyed watching Packer games with her dad since infancy. There's a photo of her at 18-months old sitting next to her daddy with her sippy cup of milk, watching the game and sharing "game day" graham crackers. By the age of four she understood that # 4 on the TV often had the football, was part of all the excitement in the show, and he was a player daddy sometimes got mad at.

"There's number four!" She'd point him out every time she watched. It was as if she felt some kind of kinship with him.

In 2003, the year Brett injured his thumb.

Anna would look for him and ask, "Is his thumb better?" She was concerned about his "owwie." There was definitely a love for the Packer QB from this little girl's end, and the family was praying that Anna's hero would feel the same about her.

He did. Arrangements were made to have the memorable encounter take place on September 24, 2003. It was a sunny, temperate day. Anna was excited to wear the Packer cheerleader outfit that Jackie from Make-A-Wish had purchased for her. Jennifer and Jeff packed up the massive amount of supplies Anna now required when leaving home – a tank of oxygen with hose and facemask, a lidocaine prescription and saline "bullets," a special nebulizing device, a handheld pulse oximeter, a bulb syringe, liquid formula, a feeding pump, an extra feeding tube button, straight catheters, and last, but certainly not least, the Brett Favre jersey in Anna's size for him to sign.

Jen and Jeff dropped off their lively one-year-old daughter Sylvia at a friend's home before embarking on the short, but all-important trip to Green Bay. The atmosphere in their minivan was an odd mix of excitement, anxiety, curiosity, but also, peace. Weeks before Jeff had had the idea of creating a "prayer card" with Anna's picture on it with a request to pray for her. They hoped to offer it to some of the players. It brought them tremendous peace thinking about how so many people would be praying for Anna.

The day's tour began when the family met Anna's "wish-makers" in the newly renovated Atrium at Lambeau Field. First stop was one of the private boxes, and then down to actually walk on the field right into the end zone. Next they toured the meeting rooms and locker room. Once inside the locker room they looked for Brett's locker. To their delight, they discovered Anna's "locker" right beside his! It was complete with her own jersey (and "Walentowski" actually fit across it!).

The whole while, Anna kept asking "Where's Brett Favre?" Finally, the family was escorted to the Don Hutson Center (across the street from Lambeau) where the team was practicing. In a matter of only a few minutes, Brett came over to meet her.

The first words out of Anna's mouth were, "Is your thumb all better?"

"Yes, it is," he smiled, holding up his thumb for her to see for herself.

The big-hearted Packer legend told her about his daughters and about how much he likes fishing for really big catfish down in Mississippi. Anna gave him a picture she'd drawn (a smiling sunflower) and then he gently played catch with her using a Nerf football. Once he had helped her back into the stroller, he willingly endured more picture taking.

Favre had no sooner returned to practice when Ryan Longwell and Rob Davis came over to tape up her wrists like theirs. When practice ended, Coach Mike Sherman invited Anna onto the field and introduced her to the players. Many of the players and several of the coaches greeted her and took a few moments to chat with her. Ahman Green, Donald Driver, Antonio Chatman, Javon Walker, Kabeer Gbaja Biamila, Doug Pederson and coach Ray Sherman were among them.

The team invited the family to stay for lunch. Olive Garden catered the food, and during the course of the meal, several of the players visited with Anna and signed her football. Many of the players asked for Anna's picture prayer card.

Al Harris leaned into Anna with a question for her.

"Will you sign my picture, Anna?"

Next, former head coach Mike Sherman asked for her autograph! What a touching way to close her time with them!

It was a full and tiring day for Anna, but somehow she found the stamina for her big event. In 2007, the family had the opportunity to meet Brett's wife, Deanna, at her book signing in Appleton. Deanna's mention of Anna in her book *Don't Bet Against Me* eventually led to a Sports Illustrated article which talked about Anna, and a second meeting with Brett.

On December 6, 2007, Brett Favre received an even more prestigious award than the Sports Illustrated Sportsman of the Year Award. He received the Chris Greicius Celebrity Award from the Make-A-Wish Foundation. It's given to entertainers and athletes who go above and beyond the norm in granting the wishes of children with life-threatening medical conditions.

The Green Bay Packers organization has granted more than 90 wishes since 1990. Meeting Brett Favre has been the wish of nearly 65 children in that time span. The award ceremony took place at Lambeau Field after practice that Thursday. Anna Walentowski, a nine-year-old from Neenah, WI, who continues her battle with a degenerative brain disorder, was on hand to witness the event. Anna first met Favre in 2004 for her Make-A-Wish request. At the time of her wish, Favre was told Anna had little time left to live.

Brett and Deanna put a picture of the little girl on their refrigerator. Deanna wrote in her book, "Every day we looked at that picture and prayed for Anna and her family." Favre teared up when he realized that Anna had survived to meet him again.

"My wish is granted," said Favre, who then had to pause for a long moment before he could continue to talk. Shaking, Favre was comforted by Anna, who turned to give him a hug.

"Congratulations," she told him.

"I'm just so happy to see her here standing beside me," Favre said.

Here is an update as of the publishing of this story. Anna has remained fairly stable medically. She still has a feeding tube used for supplements, water and a small amount of calories. She eats orally and even enjoys some school hot lunches. She has continued to grow and learn. She attends school every day, leaving early twice a week. Although she still has mobility challenges, she began using a walker at school almost two years ago. The scoliosis has continued to progress slowly, but they hope to hold off on surgery for another few years. She wears a spinal brace and is very tolerant of it.

Anna's ability to process information (sensory input) is still impaired, as is her sense of balance, but the family views all of this from the perspective of "what could have been." Infant onset Alexander Disease life span prognosis is two years of age. Juvenile onset: 7 to 10 years. Doctors believe Anna is a "cross over case" of infant and juvenile onset. The Walentowskis have not been given a clear prognosis. When the neurologist saw Anna in 2009, the family asked her if there was any insight she could offer about the onset of puberty and Anna's overall neurological pathology.

The doctor's response: "I don't know. I've not had an Alexander's patient that lived this long."

And there is one Green Bay legend that's glad she has lived long enough for him to meet her, not once, but twice.

By Steve Rose as told by Jen Walentowski

∝ ∾

Anna Walentowski, Jen Walentowski, and Brett Favre

5 Only in Green Bay

If you, like me, were growing up in South Carolina during the '60s and '70s, pro football wasn't exactly on your radar. Oh, there were the expansion Atlanta Falcons, but they might as well have been the Kenosha Maroons for all I knew. Occasionally we watched the Washington Redskins on Sundays because the old-timers assured us they were the local team for years, even if the neighborhood had a 400-mile radius.

Then, one day, I noticed my hometown paper, the *Greenville News*, was carrying a daily diary of a local guy who had been drafted in the 15th round by the Green Bay Packers. Almost no one today would remember that Dan Eckstein from tiny Presbyterian College was the last man cut by the 1969 Packers but, to me, he was a personal guide into a faraway, mythological world. Everyone on my peewee football team pretended to be Starr or Nitschke, and all of the coaches tried to yell and inspire like Lombardi, but these larger-than-life characters were like dragons and giants, unreachable and certainly unknowable, to a kid in the Deep South.

Eckstein, however, changed all that for me. Through his diary, which I read every day, the little wide receiver portrayed himself as a scared rookie initially awed by the Hall of Famers around him. Eventually he came to know them as people, and nice ones at that. I still remember his story about someone offering him a ride to practice from some place called "De Pere." Without looking before getting in, Eckstein wrote that he nearly fainted when he noticed he was sitting between Ken Bowman and Jim Weatherwax, and that the driver was none other than Ray Nitschke himself.

Of his first training-camp catch from Bart Starr, Eckstein wrote that his mother could've hauled it in.

"Nice, quick move, Dan. And good catch," Starr told him.

"To catch a pass from Bart Starr, and then to have him call me by my first name? Simply fantastic. Sometimes I think I'm in heaven. But then those practices – not exactly the way I pictured it'd be up there," Eckstein would write of that ordinary moment.

Years later, writing columns on the Packers for the Milwaukee Journal Sentinel, I tracked down Eckstein and gave him a call.

"Who would believe this," I told him. "A couple of country boys who made it all the way to Green Bay."

My experiences, minus the grass drills, were the same as his. Some of the biggest people in the NFL's most storied town were the best. For me, it started with Bob Harlan.

My first experience with the Packers was a 1990 exhibition game against my hometown Falcons at County Stadium. When I arrived at the press gate, however, there was no pass for me, so the attendant called up to the press box. Eavesdropping on the conversation, I soon learned he had Harlan on the phone. I felt like Eckstein catching a square-out from Starr. Wait, THE Bob Harlan, president of the Packers?

"Yes, I know Mike. Please, let him in," Harlan told the attendant.

I had been in town only a couple of months. I was a nobody and an outsider at that, just another face in the press gallery. I'm sure the man couldn't have picked me out of a lineup, but that was Bob Harlan. Still, it took me several years before I grasped the essence of the place that is like no other in the world.

My college roommate at the University of South Carolina, Bob Dudek, was born and raised in Green Bay. He remained in my home state as a lawyer, while I migrated to his as a sportswriter. Almost every year he comes up to visit, usually in the dead of winter, so he can sit inside Lambeau Field to remember what it was like to have a hometown team in the NFL's actual hometown, and to rib me about the fact that I had none. He would take me to his childhood home, to the corner store, to his parish school, to the streets that still looked the same now as they did then. And just beyond the treetops, there it was, one of the greatest stadiums in the world.

All the while I'm thinking, "What a great way to grow up."

Those thoughts stayed with me when I'd see the wide receiver from my school, Robert Brooks, catching a ride from practice not in the back of Nitschke's new Chevy, but on the bike of a child that could've been my roommate years ago.

I smiled while I thought, "Only in Green Bay."

I thought about it during the turbulent summer of 2008, when the town was divided over Brett Favre. Just when I thought I couldn't write another word about No. 4, there was Aaron Rodgers standing graciously against the 'boos' that soon turned to cheers. Again I smiled while I thought, "Only in Green Bay."

Eckstein's newspaper diary was eventually turned into a book called "The 41st Packer." I bought it with what was supposed to be baseball card money when it came out almost 40 years ago. It's still on my shelf.

When I see that book, I smile while I think, "Only in Green Bay!"

By Michael Hunt, Milwaukee Journal Sentinel

CR ꙮ

6 1st Lady of Lambeau

One of the most passionate Packer fans I know is Jim Coursolle. Let me rephrase that. One of the most passionate people I know is Jim, who just happens to be a Packer fan, and who went above and beyond the call of duty to show his allegiance to his favorite team. What did he do? He named the call letters of his radio station after the team! That's right. In July 1990, Packer 99.5 WPKR went on the air.

Until 2003, when Jim sold the station, the entrepreneur had the walls of the station adorned with a plethora of Packer memorabilia, including a framed ticket to the infamous Ice Bowl. The thing that caught my eye, however, was an envelope which had once contained a love letter written back in 1918.

In the late '90s Jim and Diane Coursolle's daughter, Wendy, attended St. Norberts College in De Pere, WI. If that name sounds vaguely familiar, it's because that's the venue the Packers choose each year to bunk at during the early part of training camp. Jim and Diane visited regularly to watch their daughter Wendy perform at halftime as part of the dance team for the basketball games.

"Every time we were there, I couldn't help but notice an older gentleman with white hair who always sat at the top of the bleachers. One night I decided to introduce myself."

"Hi, I'm Jim Coursolle."

"Hello, my name is Father Dennis Burke," he kindly replied.

"If you don't mind my asking, why do you sit way up here?" quizzed Jim.

"Ah, well…when you get old, it's much more comfortable to lean against the wall," he informed his new friend.

Burke went on to divulge that he was the former president of St. Norbert and quickly the conversation came to the Green Bay Packers, who play just up the road from the campus. Jim and Father Burke became very good friends over time. Upon learning of Jim's fascination with the team, Burke made a suggestion.

"Jim, I think there's a lady you should meet. Her name is Marguerite Lambeau."

Jim knew right away who she was.

"Sure. Curly Lambeau's first wife."

"That's right. She's an amazing woman," affirmed Father Burke.

In just a matter of weeks, Burke was making the introductions.

"Marguerite, I'd like you to meet Jim and Diane Coursolle."

"How nice to meet you," they each replied, extending hands to one another.

At the time of the meeting, Ms Lambeau, nearly 90 years old, was still very active and in general good health. She had been a buyer for HC Prange Company for many years, jetsetting around the nation. Marguerite Marie Van Kessel had been married to Curly Lambeau from 1919 to 1934 when they amicably divorced. They had a son, John, born in 1920.

Diane and Jim became very nurturing of Marguerite. Jim explained.

"We'd decided that Marguerite had been lost in the shuffle over the years, virtually forgotten. So we wrote a letter to the Packer organization requesting that they host a banquet to honor her. Bob (Harlan) thought it was a great idea," remembers Coursolle.

"So, we got a room at the Radisson for the banquet where Bob presented her with a plaque which read: "First Lady of Lambeau," a recognition she so rightfully deserved. It was a wonderful afternoon, one that was long overdue," finished Jim.

Over the years, Marguerite would regale the Coursolles with unknown and private stories about Curly.

"I lent Curly the first $50 for the Green Bay Packer franchise fee. He was always thinking about football. He regularly had players and coaches over for chalk talks. We wives would go upstairs and visit with one another for hours on end."

One story, in particular, epitomized Curly's infatuation with the game.

"I woke up one morning and discovered his pillow covered with X's and O's. He had diagrammed plays with a black marker," she laughed, and then continued.

"Jim and Diane, since that wonderful party for me, the sadness I've felt for so many years seems to be gone," she confided in them.

Shortly after that conversation, Marguerite began to attend Packer events again. The Packers and the Hall of Fame kept in contact with Marguerite and invited her to enjoy the home games from the luxury boxes.

"It was quite nice, but you don't see as much. I liked it better in the stands."

Marguerite remained in good health and continued to drive until September, 1997, when she fell and broke her hip. A birthday party was thrown in honor of her 100th birthday on April 30, 1999. She sat down at her piano and played a peppy version of "If You Knew Suzie." Marguerite died in 2001 while living in a nursing home. Jim and Diane visited her there often, and paid their final respects at her funeral.

The stadium at 1265 Lombardi has carried the name of her ex-husband since 1957. Interestingly, Marguerite never had a bad word to say about the man who lived in the fast lane, or as the locals said, "went

Marguerite Lambeau with Jim Coursolle

15

Hollywood."

Marguerite and Curly met at Green Bay's East High School. She was a year behind him. She looked out the window one day and spotted the rugged and dashing young man on the field.

"I thought, 'Well, there's my boyfriend.' We became friends and dated for a long time. Sometimes Curly would come by my home, behind the family grocery store, and toss pebbles at my window, and eventually we got married," she recalled fondly.

The envelope hanging on Jim's wall serves as a reminder that Curly felt the same about her.

Jim and Diane Coursolle still remember the story Marguerite tells of a love letter written by Curly to her. It portrays a side of the man that few got to see, and didn't know about.

Hopefully, you now know a bit more about his wife, who some have called "The First Lady of Lambeau."

By Steve Rose with memories from Jim Coursolle

CR ЯO

7 It's Pronounced "Ma-Cow-ski"

I grew up in Iowa and was never really a football fan when I was younger, perhaps because my dad wasn't much of a sports fan either. The closest we ever really got to the Packers was a Packers stocking cap my little brother always wore while helping with chores around the farm in the winter. He wasn't a fan, either. He just liked the colors.

Between working on our family farm, not having an in-state professional football team, and relaxing and visiting family members on Sundays, we never really got into football as kids until we were in junior high and high school. Even then, our devotion was to our local team and the Iowa Hawkeyes.

The Pack came into my life in the very early '90s when I started working part time at WKBH radio in La Crosse. I did the Sunday morning shift, playing country music, recording commercials and "ripping and reading" sports stories for the sports report every hour. In an attempt to be frugal, we didn't have a news feed system, so I would have to buy the Tribune on the way into work at 5:30 a.m. Everything we did for news, weather and sports came from that paper.

I got my first real lesson about the Packers and how sharp listeners and fans were in a most unexpected way. Here's a sound bite from the report I gave over the air.

"And the Packers quarterback, Don Magikowski, had a wonderful game yesterday as Green Bay beat the New Orleans Saints," I reported.

Actually, I read his name for months that way until, one day, when the phone rang.

"Hi, WKBH," I answered.

"Yes, this is Carl. Say, Don's name is not pronounced 'Magikowski.' The 'j' is silent,'" he kindly corrected me.

"Thanks, Carl. I appreciate that."

I confess I didn't know any better, nor did I care. It was, after all, just sports and just the Packers. We only got calls on mispronunciations of the obituaries reports. Was this Majkowski guy's family listening or something? What's the big deal?

In late 1995 I moved to Packer country. My wife and I lived in Appleton. One of her co-workers, Vicki, and her husband Ross, were die-hard Packers fans. They often invited us over to their apartment to watch the games. A few of their other close friends and Ross' brother Mark would be there, too.

I was amazed at the amount of yelling, the arguments about calls, the number of pillows and other items thrown and the profanity that was strewn together after either a bad play or a bad call by a ref. I didn't understand. What's the big deal? It's just a game, right?

That season the Pack lost the NFC championship to the Cowboys. The Appleton Post-Crescent actually devoted an entire section of the paper to dealing with depression after the loss. There were reports of high levels of absenteeism at workplaces for several days. Ross admitted feeling physically ill for nearly a week. No, he wasn't hung over. He was simply emotionally drained for days...over a game!

I didn't get it. It's a game!

Ross and Vicki eventually bought a house of their own. Then "the shrine" was built. The entire basement was turned into wall-to-wall Packers memorabilia, things that Ross had in boxes in storage at his parents' home near Sturgeon Bay, things apparently waiting to be mounted in their proper places of adornment some day.

I remember the day I finally realized that, to some people, this is more than a game. Ross had purchased what we will refer to as the "Packer Coins." These were some type of gold coin to commemorate the 1996 Super Bowl win.

At the time, their cash flow was tight. Ross was in between jobs and they really didn't have the money he dumped into these coins. Vicki was upset and it came up in conversation one night as we were out together enjoying some adult beverages.

"Hey, these coins are an investment," Ross contended.

I laughed. Correction. I more than laughed. I razzed, cajoled, belittled and berated.

"If you want to spend money on things like that, hey it's your money. But please don't insult the rest of the thinking world by telling me these coins are an investment."

I hurt Ross' feelings so deeply that we didn't speak for nearly a month. When we finally talked again, he shared his heart.

"Robbie, I know you don't understand my love for this team," he told me.

He was right. I didn't. I thought it was borderline mental illness, or the result of years of heavy drinking, but I was impressed with his stories. We talked for hours. Suffice it to say, he went on to explain that his childhood, and life in general in Wisconsin, revolved around the Packers. They were the glue that seemed to hold everyone together.

After Ross & Vicki had their first child, and we had our first child, the Sunday parties slowed down substantially. I think about Ross and Vicki often, and wonder if that same indoctrination of love for their team is being instilled into their children. I'm going to hazard a guess and say the answer is 'yes.'

I currently work as a talk show host for an affiliate station for the Packers Radio Network in Appleton on 1150 WHBY. I spent time in the bar business before getting back into radio, and I have seen some extremely intense Packers fans. I've followed the team partly out of necessity, but the more I see how the fans literally love this team, the more I slowly understand. You'll now find me in front of a TV or else listening to the game on the radio every Sunday.

That said, you'll never find in my basement a 'shrine' like Ross has in his. However, I recently went to see a good friend of mine in Minnesota who has a Vikings shrine. The one Ross has is much better.

My best friend is a Packers fan and he loves coming to Lambeau. He's been a fan since childhood, but he feels "it" when he comes to Green Bay. Unfortunately, my closest cousins are Vikings fans. My sister also married a Vikings fan. He is a nice enough guy, but he has, sadly, indoctrinated my sister, nephews and my niece into a purple and gold cult. You can imagine the amount of flack I get from them on game days.

They can wear their team's gear. They can go to games. They can even win a game or two. They can try to equal what the fans in Green Bay have, but they won't come close, and they will never be as devoted as Packer fans are.

Here, it's a whole different breed. It's more than game. It's a way of life...so much so that they even know how to pronounce their heroes' names.

By Robbie Johnson

CR SO

8 Ryan Longwell Kicked Me in the Head

All Anna Romenesko, 11, wanted to do was spend some time at Lambeau Field with her family. Was that asking too much? It was Family Night, August 5, 2005. Anna was sitting in the front row in an end zone section of this historic venue with her 14-year-old brother, Sam, and her parents Paul and Carol. Quiet, somewhat shy, and tiny, Anna was just minding her own business when Ryan Longwell kicked her in the head! Well, in a manner of speaking.

Each year, the week before Packer pre-season starts, the team has Family

Night. Tickets are sold at a very affordable price so that families who wouldn't normally be able to come to a game during the pre or regular season can have an opportunity to watch their team play. The Intra Squad game sets up offensive players to go up against defensive players. Afterward, a drawing takes place for the players to give their jerseys to the fans. The evening culminates in a firework display.

There were a total of 24 family members in attendance. Everyone was having a great time enjoying the pregame festivities when, suddenly, kerplunk! Anna had been hit on the top right of her head by a Ryan Longwell practice field goal! Normally, a net up is put up to protect against a happening like this, but, for whatever reason, it had not been working that day. Actually, this was the second ball that came into the stands, the first one landing safely between spectators. Needless to say, Anna was startled and injured, but she never forgot that moment.

"It really surprised me. I didn't know what happened until I saw the ball bounce into the seats in back of us," she recalls.

"Oh honey! Are you okay?" Anna's mom inquired immediately.

She wasn't. Anna began to cry, not so much because it hurt (although it did), but more because it had startled her. One of the Packer staff who was working with Ryan came over to retrieve the ball and realized Anna had been hit. A few moments later, realizing she was still crying, he came back and presented her with the ball. Anna's quick-thinking mom had an idea. Grandma Sievers, Anna's maternal grandmother, was working in the concessions that night.

"Let's go to get you some ice from Grandma."

It was quite some distance from where the Romeneskos were sitting to where Grandma was working. Grandma noticed, the moment they arrived, that something was amiss.

"My goodness! What in the world happened?" she inquired.

"Can we get some ice for Anna? She just got hit in the head by a ball," explained Anna's mom.

"Oh, honey. Let's get some ice on that bump," Grandma replied tenderly.

Ryan, who now had heard about the incident, came to the stands to apologize and to sign the ball. Family members still in the stands explained that she and her mom went to visit grandma to get ice for the bump on her head. Ryan promised that he'd return later.

Moments later Anna, back in her seat with her mom, was holding a latex glove filled with ice against her head. Her aunts, uncles and cousins couldn't wait to tell her about her missed opportunity with Ryan. Shortly after, the staff member who originally gave Anna the ball returned.

"I'm going to take the ball to Ryan and have him autograph it for you. What's your name?" he asked. When he finally returned, he was carrying the autographed football.

"Ryan will come over after the game. He wants to talk to you," he assured Anna.

Anna held onto the ball with all her might, even passing on an offer from one man who was willing to pay her $100 for the autographed ball.

Only a few minutes after the team had finished their scrimmage, a jersey-less #8 came walking toward the Romenesko section. He looked at Anna.

"I'm so sorry, Anna," he said apologetically.

"It's okay. I know you didn't mean to do it, it was just an accident," she said with a quiver of forgiveness in her voice and a slight smile across her face.

Longwell pulled from a pocket a silver marker and, as promised, autographed the ball. He made a point of staying to visit with the family for a while, chatting with them as well as others who were still lingering in the stands. It's no surprise that, in what would be Ryan's last season in Green Bay, he became very special to a little girl from Kimberly.

"He was my favorite player after that," said the now 17-year-old.

All is certainly forgiven, but not at all forgotten. Anna's memory of that night is as clear as it was the night she got the knot on her head.

I suppose it

Kicker Ryan Longwell laughs with Anna Romenesko

could be assumed that Longwell bolted for the Minnesota Vikings for more money in Free Agency. One might wonder, however. Could it be possible that the word got around town that Longwell kicked a little 11-year-old in the head one summer night in August of 2005 inside Lambeau Field and was run out of town?

That question will, undoubtedly, go unanswered, but we certainly hope Ryan has changed his ways and "looks both ways before he kicks," and that he was truly sincere in his apology to the little girl who never expected she'd be leaving Titletown with a bump on her noggin.

Cradling an autographed football on the way back to Kimberly, however, undoubtedly made bearing her headache just a bit easier.

By Steve Rose with memories from Anna Romenesko

ॐ ঙ

9 Cruisin' for Cancer Packer Style

Although you've seen him on television many times, you probably never noticed him because of who he was walking beside. Green Bay Packers Senior Security Director Jerry Parins could always be found walking beside Brett Favre. At the end of each game, it was Jerry's responsibility to see that Favre was afforded safe passage to the sanctuary of the locker room, maneuvering the MVP and Pro Bowl quarterback through the postgame on-field gauntlet of media, awe-struck opposing players, and any three-piece-suited VIPs longing for a word or handshake. Jerry was Brett's bodyguard in the most literal sense, as evidenced by Jerry's book aptly titled, Bodyguard to the Packers.

What Jerry couldn't have anticipated was it would be he who needed a "bodyguard," otherwise know in medical circles as oncologists. Jerry Parins was diagnosed with colon cancer. The diagnosis would prove life altering, not just for Jerry, but for hundreds, perhaps thousands, of people battling cancer. Once Jerry came to terms with his own personal battle, he asked himself a challenging question. How could he turn a big negative into an even bigger positive? Borne from that question came the Jerry Parins Cruise for Cancer. Jerry's dream was to hold a massive motorcycle ride fundraiser. All profits would be distributed to several local organizations that directly help cancer patients and their families with their struggles.

Jerry began to marshal the considerable resources available only to a person in his professional position and, in the process, Jerry's past caught up with him. The respect he had garnered throughout the entire National Football League exploded into a blitz of assistance, not just from the Green Bay Packers, but from Seattle to San Francisco, New York to New Orleans, Tampa Bay to Tennessee and, yes, even from the despised Minnesota Vikings and Chicago Bears!

On the morning of Saturday, June 12, 2004, the sun-drenched parking lot of Lambeau Field took on a carnival atmosphere. Bikers riding everything from Harleys to Hondas streamed in by the hundreds. Huge, white, open-air tents were erected in the parking lot. Under one tent, volunteers served coffee as well as baked goods donated by Starbucks and Bake My Day. Under a tent positioned near the stadium entrance was the main stage where hard and heavy music blared from the deejay's powerful speaker system. Beneath the two largest tents were the items for both the live and silent auctions. Helmets, jerseys, footballs and photographs, all had been donated and autographed by seemingly every star player in the entire NFL! It was the motherlode of Memorabilia!

Volunteers worked their way through the crowd selling raffle tickets. Radio stations broadcasted live from the event. The newspaper photographer clicked away and local TV stations were busy conducting interviews and videotaping all the festivities for that evening's newscasts. This frenzy of activity would continue until 10:30 a.m., at which time the formal pre-ride ceremony at the main stage would take place. Mine was the privilege of emceeing the event, and upon getting the attention of the hundreds of bikers, the people and bikes fell silent as I introduced Packers Chaplain Fr. Jim Baraniak to open the ceremony with a prayer. Father Jim was followed by words of thanks and encouragement from Packers President Bob Harlan and team Chief Operating Officer John Jones.

My colleague, WFRV-TV 5 Sports Director Larry McCarren then stepped up to introduce five Packers players who were in attendance.

Larry, a 12-year Packer veteran and former All-Pro center, provided insight, lightheartedness and comedy as he portrayed the human side of each of the hulking, sheepish players. It was then time to introduce the star of the show, Jerry Parins, who gave a moving, heartfelt thank-you to all who came. That Jerry was overwhelmed at the turnout for the first-ever Jerry Parins 'Cruise for Cancer' would be an understatement.

Jerry then took the ceremony one emotional step further when he invited to the stage four cancer patients he had met and befriended in the hospital oncology unit. Ranging in ages from 10 to 67, Jerry's special guests would join the hundreds of bikers on the ride which would take them from Lambeau Field north to Peshtigo to Vandervest Harley Davidson for raffles, games and food, and then back to Lambeau Field later in the day for the auctions, music and more festivities.

Jerry knew that these four people, weakened by chemotherapy treatments, could not physically withstand the rigors of a 40-mile motorcycle ride, so he arranged for the Harley Davidson limousine to chauffeur his friends all day long! Picture a 40-foot-long black stretch Hummer, and you've got a pretty good idea of what this awesome, stunning vehicle looked like.

What I will most remember from that day is something that happened about an hour before the ceremony, long before the speeches, the player introductions, the limo ride or the sight and sound of a thousand motorcycles firing up simultaneously. Just before 10 a.m., Jerry walked up to me and grabbed my arm. He had something to tell me.

"Tom, I need your help with something. Follow me. But I don't want any media."

It was clear that Jerry was on a mission so I followed obediently. Some of Jerry's staffers had gathered together the four cancer patients and their families. We totaled about 25. Jerry led us through gates and security guards. The Packers Senior Security Director wields that kind of power! Suddenly, we found ourselves in the bowels of Lambeau Field, the loading area, an underground bunker large enough for trucks and heavy equipment, where food and supplies are delivered and where limousines chauffeur in the likes of John Madden, Al Michaels and superstar players who would otherwise be mobbed by adoring fans.

Having been here many times as emcee of various Packer events I knew we were walking toward "The Tunnel," the hallowed passageway through which Packers of the Glory Years and beyond entered the playing field. I thought perhaps Jerry was going to lead us all into the tunnel and onto the field which would have been quite the treat for any Packer fan. I was wrong. We walked past "The Tunnel," through wooden double doors and down a carpeted hallway. At another set of double doors stood two Packers security employees who, upon seeing Jerry and his entourage, dutifully swung the doors open.

Immediately I realized we were being escorted into the inner sanctum, the place no lay person is allowed, the place no fan has ever walked, the place where only Packer players and coaches are allowed. On this day, however, Jerry Parins' special cancer friends were granted passage into the locker room of the Green Bay Packers! There, waiting for all of us, were Bob Harlan, John Jones and players Aaron Kampman, Kabeer Gbaja Biamila and Ahman Green. Jerry's friends and their families were absolutely stunned as they looked around the football-shaped room at the names of their player heroes on placards above each locker.

But where was Brett Favre's locker? His was the first locker, but his name wasn't there. The players' names were also missing from above lockers two, three and four. But wait. There were names above the four lockers, the names of Jerry's four cancer friends! Hanging inside each locker was a Packer game jersey with each friend's name on the back. The number on the jersey was the friend's age! Each locker shelf was loaded with several autographed items and souvenirs! Bob Harlan welcomed everyone to this special place. Then it was Jerry's turn, and in typical Jerry style, he deflected all accolades from himself and instead thanked the Packers and thanked his special friends and their families for being there, not just 'there' as in the locker room, but for being there for each other as they all fought the battle against this ominous foe together.

It was time to leave. One thousand bikers were waiting outside for the 10:30 ceremony to begin. I grabbed the microphone.

"Friends, I wish each and every one of you could have seen what I've just seen."

As a postscript to this story, at this writing, we are about to hold the 7th annual Jerry Parins Cruise for Cancer. Just last week, Jerry handed out the money we raised last year, $84,000, to eight local cancer support organizations, Fund for Children With Cancer, The Bellin Health Foundation, Community Memorial Hospital, Families of Children With

Cancer, Inc., The Leukemia and Lymphoma Society, St. Vincent Hospital Regional Cancer Center Compassionate Care Fund, St. Vincent Hospital Regional Cancer Center Comfort Capes Program and Unity.

To date, the Jerry Parins Cruise for Cancer has raised more than $300,000. Wherever you may be, why not stop around next time and do some Cruisin' for Cancer, and do it with style – Packer Style!

By Tom Zalaski, WFRV-TV 5, Green Bay

ℭℜ ℬℴ

Tom Zalaski emcees Cruisin' for Cancer

10 Bernardo: A Good Kid & Big Grin

The boss called me into his palatial glass office back in 1997 and informed me he wanted a story on Packers middle linebacker Bernardo

Harris. Naturally, I asked him what "the hook" was. The Packers, a year removed from winning Super Bowl XXXI, were returning to Harris' home state of North Carolina to play the Panthers that week. That was it. Immediately, I turned and rolled my eyes. Sometimes you can make chicken salad out of chicken doo-doo, and sometimes you can't. I didn't have much hope for this story, unless any of our readers were suffering from insomnia.

Bernardo was a nice enough guy, but a quiet one. Never had much to say, at least nothing you'd want to scribble into your notebook. Not his fault; that's just who he was. And I was supposed to write our main Sunday sports story about a guy with nothing to say returning to his home state to play a football game? Really?

So I headed to my desk, grabbed the Packers' media guide and starting reading. Then I began to make some calls. I found his high school football coach at Chapel Hill High School, Bill Hodgin, who began to share a remarkable story. He told me how many years ago, out of the Carolina blue, he got a call from a young kid.

"Coach," the little guy said, "can I come out and eat with y'all?"

"Sure, don't see why not," he replied.

So 12-year-old Bernardo Harris started showing up to the local restaurant each Friday to join in the pre-game meal. Then he'd hop on the bus and do whatever he could to help the team on the sideline during the game. Then the team would return to school and young Bernardo would disappear into the night, all by himself.

"When I began asking questions about him, I knew he was better spending time with us. He needed to be with us.''

It was an all-too-familiar sad story. Harris grew up in a neighborhood where "crack" was king, guns were a given and gangs often provided the only family structure some kids knew. His mom died when he was young. His dad wasn't in the picture. He was being raised by his great-grandmother. But this story didn't turn out like so many others. Whether it was divine intervention, luck, sheer will, or his intuitive ability to know right from wrong, Harris not only survived, but prospered.

"He had a tremendous focus on what he wanted to do,'' said Hodgin. "Almost like tunnel vision.''

Harris wanted to be a football player. When his career concluded at Chapel Hill High School, he earned a scholarship to North Carolina. The kid who had suffered so much never allowed his trials to rule his life. He was Mr. Happy Go Lucky, always smiling, making friends with everyone with whom he came in contact.

"He always had that big ol' grin on his face. Everyone in town loved him," said Becky Medford, administrative assistant to then Tar Heels coach Mack Brown. "And Chapel Hill's not a huge place."

His Tar Heel career was solid, and the Kansas City Chiefs signed him as a free agent in 1994. But he injured his knee the first week of training camp and, once healed, was released. So he returned to Chapel Hill, worked in the parts department at a local BMW dealership, and every day after work went home and worked out. He believed in himself. His wife, Kellie, believed in him. Finally, so did the Packers, who signed him as a free agent in 1995.Though it appeared his hard work would go for naught when he broke his arm during training camp, he had shown the Packers enough that they decided to keep him around.

Harris became a special teams whiz in '96 and the following year with starter George Koonce out with a knee injury and incumbent Ron Cox sent packing, Harris inherited the job by default. But there was no fault in his play. The starting middle linebacker job was his.

Harris may have escaped his roots, but he never forgot them. He continued to return to Chapel Hill to participate in a Hometown Heroes program in Durham, a free football camp for area youth, and did whatever else he could to improve his old neighborhood.

"Bernardo is something special. He's excelled personally and professionally at all levels. And he's been able to maintain a degree of humility," commented his agent James Williams.

Harris not only saved himself, but he was determined to help save others, too. His first mission was to take one of his cousins out of Chapel Hill, and bring him to Green Bay to live with him and his family so he'd have a better chance to succeed.

"Bernardo's a young man with old-man responsibilities, if you know what I mean," Williams said.

It was after the Super Bowl when Harris returned to see his old pals at the BMW dealership in Chapel Hill. His co-workers always asked him, and teased him, about his routine of working all day and working out all night. He brought along something to show them: his Super Bowl ring.

"It was so I wouldn't have to ever go back," Harold Ayscue, Harris' boss, recalled Harris saying.

"And," Ayscue added, "He had that big ol' grin on his face."

What was a seemingly unremarkable assignment turned into a remarkable story thanks to a guy with a good head and an even better heart. It served, and still does serve, as a reminder that football is just a game. It's what you do in life, and what people will remember long after the uniform comes off for the final time, that really matters.

By Mike Woods, Appleton Post-Crescent

CR SO

11 Tommy Helps Save the Pack

When Wisconsin Governor Tommy Thompson's phone rang, he answered it. He answered in a big way.

"Governor Thompson?"

"Yes."

"It's Bob Harlan from the Green Bay Packers calling."

"Yes, my friend, how can I help you?"

The explanation was something that would take a while.

Tommy Thompson served as the 42nd Governor of Wisconsin, otherwise known by its residents as Packerland. He was also President George W. Bush's Health and Human Service Secretary until 2005.

Tommy Thompson was born at home in 1941, a common practice then. His father, Allen, ran a gas station and grocery store. His mother, Julia, was a teacher. Tommy grew up in a poor family, but like many families, both rich and poor, his became knit into the fabric of the Green Bay Packers.

"Every family in the '60s planned Thanksgiving dinner around the Packers and Lions game. That was a big thing," recalls the former Governor.

There is one memory that he laughs about, which, at the time, wasn't nearly as funny as it is today.

"My sister, Juliann, got two tickets to the Ice Bowl of 1967, but instead of taking me, she took her boyfriend. As it turned out, I was at home with some heat, and she was, quite literally, out in the cold. All she could say afterward was, 'It was so cold you wouldn't believe it,'" he chuckled.

Thompson has had a variety of opportunities to meet many of the Packers he had watched, Paul Hornung, Jim Taylor, Ray Nitschke, Boyd Dowler, Max McGee, Fuzzy Thurston, Bob Long, and even a quarterback from Mississippi a few years after. The late Reggie White walked the halls of the capitol with Thompson, and there was one player Tommy knew before he was a Packer.

"I bartended in Madison at the Varsity Tavern with Ken Bowman who went on to play for the Packers after going to the University there."

Brett Favre stepped out of the pocket to help Thompson during a gubernatorial campaign and, later, invited him to take a special trip with him.

"Brett took me deer hunting in Hayward (northern WI). There were a couple of other players along. We had a great time."

Thompson recalls another memorable moment.

"It was the last game of the 2006 season and the Packers were playing the Bears at Soldier Field. I was a presidential candidate, so I had secret service guys with me. It didn't seem to faze Brett. He invited me and my entire entourage into the locker room to introduce me to the guys. That was great."

Tommy admired former Packer GM Ron Wolf, and was able to have dinner with him during the time he was working for President Bush in Washington. Arguably, however, Thompson's finest hour politically was with the work he put in after receiving that phone call from Bob Harlan in 2000.

"Governor, we've come to the conclusion that we're going to have to renovate Lambeau Field in order to increase revenue. We need your help in allowing us to do a tax in Brown County," Harlan explained.

"Bob, I'll do whatever I can to help you," pledged Thompson.

The two worked diligently with the legislature and in 2003 the Packers, without missing a beat, began play after a $295 million development, assuring the team's financial survival for generations to come.

Tommy Thompson often set his sights on saving Wisconsin taxpayers' money whenever possible, but his greatest save may have come in tandem with Bob Harlan and the legislature of the state is home to the greatest team in all of professional sports.

"We love our Green Bay Packers and I am proud to have been a part of the process that helped to keep them here," says the former Governor proudly.

Governor, we, the fans, are glad that you and Bob were able to pull off one of the greatest rescue acts in the history of Wisconsin sports.

By Steve Rose with memories from Tommy Thompson

CR &O

12 Still Waters

Ask anyone who's old enough to remember where he was when he first heard that President John F. Kennedy, Robert Kennedy or Martin Luther King had been assassinated, and there won't be a moment's hesitation to give an answer. These were only three of the many significant and consequential moments in the history of our nation, but the shock of such moments registers a permanent memory.

Ask any Packer fan where he was in early spring of '08 when he first heard of Favre's impending retirement, and not only will you get an immediate response, it's likely to be a volatile one, at that.

While certainly that event is by no means anywhere near the equivalent of such impactful events like the deaths of leaders in our nation, Favre's decision was of paramount importance and consequence to the Packer nation, and the grief was just as palpable as if there had been a death in the family.

It might surprise you to know that, though I'm co-author of this book, I don't consider myself a die-hard Packer fan. Actually, I'm a transplant from Michigan, via a childhood spent in Illinois. It became clear, early in my marriage to Steve, that it would be prudent to ally my loyalties to his, which are green and gold through and through.

I admit that, for the most part, I refused to engage or enmesh myself in the ceaseless bantering and arguing connected to the controversy of No. 4's on-and-off-and-on again retirement from the Pack. I also avoided, whenever possible, the rabid ranting about the way the management should or should not have handled the entire affair.

Did I have some opinions on either of those matters? Of course, I had – strong ones at that. The contentiousness of everyone's opinions created an environment where clear and definitive battle lines were being drawn, an environment of which I simply did not want to be a part.

The battle raged on, even after Brett signed with the Jets. Meanwhile, I was more focused on what was happening off the field, rather than the on-the-field drama, and was far more intrigued with someone else who was caught in the fray.

Aaron Rodgers was, I initially thought, conspicuously silent during the melee. Certainly, I presumed, he'd want to engage in some kind of conversation in order to defend himself and his reputation. After all, it's difficult to be provable, testable, or show your potential skills and durability, all of which came into question, if you've never been given much of an opportunity to do so. No one would argue that point, nor would anyone argue that, caught in the very dominant shadow of Favre, the opportunity would ever be there.

Still, Rodgers said nothing.

On those rare occasions when someone was able to get a microphone in his face, his response was brief and he handled himself with poise, maturity and civility, rare qualities for most who are caught in the limelight these days, but particularly so for a "youngster" in his mid 20s.

I've heard it said that success tries the mettle of a man far more than failure, so when Aaron made his debut against the Vikings on home territory, and handed them a 24-19 defeat, I watched. I listened. His post-game interview was straightforward, honest and seasoned with a generous portion of humility.

Over the next two seasons, whether the Pack won or lost, Aaron continued to handle himself, both on and off the field, like the professional, disciplined man of integrity I believed him to be.

In preparation for this chapter, I decided to Google Aaron Rodgers, but not for his stats, personal or professional. I was looking for that "something" to confirm what I already knew, what my gut was telling me, that there was more to Aaron Rodgers than meets the eye.

I found it. Fox6Now sportscaster, Jen Lada, had been assigned to cover Aaron Rodgers' charity event at Mo's A Place for Steaks in Milwaukee on May 17, 2010. The MACC Fund was founded to work toward eradicating childhood cancer and blood disorders. According to Lada's report, "In a world where many athletes regurgitate canned and rehearsed responses, the Packers quarterback was refreshingly candid."

The clincher, the piece de resistance, for me was the ending to her report.

"My friend, the father of that young girl who passed (away), was there that night. He was one of several attendees brought up on stage where he caught a football thrown by the quarterback of the Green Bay Packers.

He asked Aaron to sign the football he'd caught. He wondered if he'd make it out to his daughter. It isn't shocking that Rodgers obliged. What caught me off guard was the dedication he made. It wasn't until after Aaron left that I first saw the autograph…and the simple yet sweet message that brought tears to this father's eyes: 'To Cheri the angel. Save me a spot. Aaron Rodgers.'" (To see the article in its entirety, go to www.fox6now.com.)

Add to Aaron's already lengthy list of admirable traits, compassion.

Most sports pundits seem to agree that Quarterback Aaron Rodgers is expected to only get better as he gleans more experience and hones his skills. What Aaron will bring to Lambeau Field, and to the world of football at large, remains to be seen, and I leave those assessments to those who are more qualified than I to make.

I'm far more interested in what goes on in the world that exists outside the walls of Lambeau Field. If what we've seen from Aaron so far is any indication, I think the world is in for quite a blessing.

By Kathi Rose

CR EO

13 Blowing Don's Horn

I was a fifth grader, deeply engrossed in the Sunday, September 27, 1970 Packer game. The play-by-play was being announced through the voice of legend Ray Scott. This particular game was becoming a nail biter, and would come down to depending on Bart Starr's backup, Don Horn, Vince Lombardi's last #1 pick in 1967.

I remember vividly only one play from the game, but it was the biggest play of the day. Don graciously filled in the details for me.

With less than two minutes left, the Packers trailed the visiting Atlanta Falcons 24-20. Norm Van Brocklen's team was on the verge of handing the Packers their second straight setback to begin the season. Coach Phil Bengston had taken out Bart Starr midway through the third quarter and replaced him with the fourth year QB Horn. Things had not been going very well for the 25-year-old that day. He missed on each of his seven passes, two of them becoming interceptions.

Just before the drive began, Packer right tackle Forrest Gregg indicated to Horn that he didn't know how long he was going to be able to keep the tough Atlanta defensive end Claude Humphrey out of the offensive backfield… not good news for the team who would have to pass the ball if there was any hope to win. The Pack began on their own 11-yd-line. Don had received a nudge from receiver, flanker Carroll Dale, after leaving the huddle, where it had been disclosed they would be running a "Fan Flat 6 Pass."

"Look at me all the way…pump…wait… and then throw the ball as far and as hard as you can to me," Dale instructed.

Don nodded and the plan and play were on. The ball was snapped. Horn dropped back, pump faked, and Falcon Kenny Reeves took the bait, bit, and bit hard, leaving Dale racing wide open down field. The ball nearly hit the clouds, soaring about 65-yards in the air. Eventually it was pulled in by Dale to score the winning touchdown. It was Horn's only completion of the day. With the victory in the books, Don had one walk he needed to take and one conversation he needed to have before the day would be complete.

Horn ambled over to the Falcon sidelines to chat with Coach Norm Van Brocklen, who had been one of Don's idols while playing for his home state Rams, but the coach was none too thrilled to see the current Packer hero.

"What the h*** was that, you lucky son-of-a b****?" referring to the winning pass Horn had just thrown. Van Brocklin was well into one of his infamous verbal assaults, all-too-common to his Falcon players.

Don initially was a bit stunned, and certainly a bit hurt. He did, however, let the coach continue to vent before getting to the reason he had wandered over to the bench in the first place.

"Coach, I need to tell you, you're my hero."

After that comment, Van Brocklin exploded and continued his verbal insults towards Don and the Packers. Unfortunately, Van Brocklin thought Don was just being sarcastic, and offered some commentary to that effect, though Horn couldn't have been more sincere in that moment. That last throw was one of Don's finest moments. Perhaps his idol didn't think so, but the fans certainly let Horn know he was their hero for the day. Ultimately, Don figured, that was good enough.

It's been nearly 40 years since his Packer playing days, but Don still talks about the excitement he felt when he was drafted by the Green Bay Packers as their first-round draft choice, with a contract for $15,000, considered to be good money back then.

"That was over $1,000 a month, something today's players wouldn't even cross the street for. People ask Don, "What is the big difference in the game today compared to then.

"Two reasons. The first is most of us had an off season job and the second is we never ran out of bounds."

Don Glenn Horn returns to Green Bay for reunions from time to time and still feels like one of the guys. He feels fortunate to have been a small part of the legendary Packer teams of the '60s.

"The fans in Green Bay are so incredible. Even if you were only here on the team for four or five years, they treat you as if you're still playing. It's like when you're once a Packer, you're always a Packer."

And the Packers got their fair share of "return" on Horn, too, especially on September 27, 1970. It's been many years since that fateful play, but both Don's memory as a player, and mine as a 10-year-old fifth grader, has not faded. Some things you just don't forget.

By Steve Rose with help from Don Horn

CR SO

14 A Patriot's Last Fling

Mike and Jane Janse ushered in the second day of the 21st century with a trip 30 miles due north of their Appleton home. The destination was none other than Lambeau Field to take in a home game.

They settled into their season ticket seats, anxious to see the game get underway. During the first quarter, Mike went to the concession stand for the usual supply of hot dogs, popcorn and refreshments. He juggled the snacks gingerly, fully aware that one misstep could culminate in an expensive mess. He was making his way through the concourse, ready to go down the stairs and back to his seat, when suddenly he looked up to see a "brown blur" coming straight toward his head! He ducked.

"Geez!" he shouted.

Peering over his shoulder, he noticed it was a football that had nearly decapitated him.

"Where in the world did that come from?" he wondered.

He stopped and turned long enough to see the ball come to a rest a short distance behind him. A stadium usher picked up the ball and walked away with it.

As he made his way back to his seat, he could hear the roar of the home crowd yelling, "Throw it back! Throw it back!" As is custom at some baseball games, if the opponent hits a home run into the hometown stands, there's usually a roaring request for it to be returned to the field, a refusal of the souvenir, if you will. Apparently, that's what the fans were chanting with regard to the football.

"What was that all about?" he asked Jane.

"One of their guys just intercepted a pass and then threw it into the stands."

"Man, that ball just about took my head off!"

"I think they're yelling for someone in the crowd to throw the ball back on the field," Jane clarified.

Without much thought, Mike suddenly bolted from his seat.

"Where you going?" Jane asked with a more-than-puzzled expression across her face.

"Be right back," he assured her as he hustled back up the steps toward the spot from which he had come just a few moments earlier. He found the usher who had picked up the football only moments earlier.

"Sir, where did you take the ball that you found up here?" he asked.

"It's in the lost and found."

"Do you mind if I have it?"

"Don't see why not."

When Mike arrived back at his seat, the football was clutched securely in his hands. Then he asked a question of the fans seated directly behind him.

"Hey, you wouldn't know who made that interception, would you?" The name they mentioned was not one Mike recognized, but at least he was holding a souvenir from this memorable game.

This particular game day was a wintry one, making it especially difficult for the visitors. The home team had annihilated the warm weather foe 49-24. One of the only real highlights for the losers was when their defensive back chucked that ball into the stands, the one Mike now cradled under his arms until he could put it in a trophy case in the family room.

The day after the game Mike picked up the sports section hoping to see if there was any mention of the player who had made the interception. Sure enough, it was the same name he'd been given the day before by the fans sitting behind him at the game.

In April of 2004, Mike was watching the national news when he heard a name that sounded vaguely familiar to him. The TV anchor spoke of a man who had turned down millions of dollars to continue to play football, and instead had chosen to enlist in the Army to serve his country. It was then that Mike realized that the ball that had been thrown into the stands four years earlier had been thrown by a patriot. Now the puzzle pieces were coming together.

"Could it be?" he wondered.

After some research, Mike came to the conclusion that his encounter with the man who had his fling that day in 2000 was one and the same as the man to whom the TV anchor had been referring, no longer a football player, but an American hero. The former Arizona Cardinals defensive back's name was Pat Tillman.

Corporal Pat Tillman died during combat defending his country's freedom while fighting in Afghanistan on April 22, 2004. The man who threw the interception caught by Pat was none other than the great Brett

Favre.

At one point in Pat Tillman's NFL career, from 1998-2001, he was given the opportunity for a five-year, $9 million contract offer from the St. Louis Rams, but he turned it down because of his loyalty to the Arizona Cardinals.

And it is at this time that we would like to express on behalf of not only the Packer fans, but fans all over the world our deepest gratitude to Patrick Tillman. To his family God bless you…and God bless the United States of America.

In Memoriam to Pat Tillman, November 6, 1976 – April 22, 2004

By Steve Rose with memories from Mike Janse

CR ЄO

15 Starr for the Course

Bart Starr believed he had let his golf partners down. He simply wasn't playing at the top of his game. He needed to apologize for not hitting a good golf shot, so that's exactly what he did to the leader of the foursome, Jim Clemons.

"I couldn't believe it. My childhood hero was apologizing to me," recalls Jim.

The Hall of Fame tourney took place at The Bull in Sheboygan. It's a really tough course and the event was a scramble. The thing that impressed Clemmy most was the way the former two-time Super Bowl MVP and Packer legend paid attention to those around him.

"Bart is the personification of what a gentleman is. When he thought no one was watching, he'd seek out the volunteers at each hole, look them square in the eye, and thank them for their participation. 'These events don't happen without people like you,'" he'd say to them.

Bart's sense of generosity and kindness were in full display as he

GREEN BAY PACKERS
HALL OF FAME GOLF CLASSIC
JULY 13, 2009 - THE BULL, SHEBOYGAN FALLS

HUMANA
Guidance when you need it most

Standing left to right: Lon Wendt, Mike Miller, Greg Biese, Bart Starr, Jim Clemons

gladly went the extra mile to indulge the requests others made of him.

"Everyone knew Bart was going to be on the course. They all had a picture or something that they wanted him to sign, or to have their picture taken with him. He never said 'no' to any of them. Trouble was, it was delaying things. That was when Bart came to me to apologize."

"Jim, I'm not playing the greatest right now. I was in a car accident a couple of weeks ago, and I guess I'm just not 100% yet," confessed Starr.

"That's okay. We weren't expecting much from a 17th round draft choice."

Jim's spontaneous come-back made Starr grin so widely he could have eaten a banana sideways.

"C'mon, Jim, why don't you join me in the cart for a while? I think we've got a lot to talk about," Bart chuckled.

Holes in one or balls in the rough, Bart Starr has been, and always will be, a "Starr for the Course."

By Steve Rose with memories from Jim Clemons

෴ ෴

16 Dennis is Blessed

I grew up in Hartford, WI, watching Packers games every Sunday. My parents would often say that I learned to count by memorizing the Packers players and their uniform numbers. I was five at the time of the Ice Bowl and it's the first game I remember watching. My dad, brother and I would tend to get a little emotional during the games. My mom, who passed away in 2008, would often go to the other room.

"If it upsets you that much, why don't you turn it off?!" she'd tell us.

One of my early memories of the Packers was when their off-season basketball team came to play at Hartford High School. I remember that I got Doug Hart's autograph.

"Hey Tiger," he called me.

I'm sure he called every kid that but I was convinced it was his personal nickname for me.

Bart Starr has a unique place in my image of the Packers. In my formative years, he was in the twilight of his career. I remember him getting sacked a lot. Then, he was the Packers coach for a long period of time that spanned from my junior high through college years. Over time, as I studied his playing career and got a chance to interview him several times. I hold him up as the ideal standard for the Green Bay Packers. "Experts" always want to minimize his role in the Packers five NFL championships and I think he has been shortchanged in NFL history. More important than his on-field success, in my opinion, is the way that he has conducted himself. His work for causes like Rawhide is truly inspirational and provides an example of using your sports platform to help others.

My first extended interview with a Packers player was while I was studying Radio-TV at UW-Oshkosh in the early 1980's. For one of our college shows, I interviewed then-Packers linebacker John Anderson. He could not have been more gracious. I'm happy to say that I've gotten to know John a little through the years and he's perhaps the most genuine pro athlete I've ever dealt with. He's a humble man who doesn't flaunt his past success and is more interested in his faith and family than being a "star".

I started covering the Packers on a regular basis in 1987 when I was hired by WTMJ-TV in Milwaukee. Later that year, I was given the opportunity by WTMJ Radio to work on the "Packers Sunday" postgame show with Brian Manthey. I've been blessed to have a chance to cover many Packers games through the years, including the Super Bowl XXXI victory in New Orleans and the Super Bowl XXXII loss in San Diego. I haven't always succeeded, but I've tried to remember how lucky and privileged I've been to have the Packers sports casting opportunities I've had. I'm well aware that many fans would give anything to trade places with me. It helps me sometimes to see people from other states and other countries touring Lambeau Field for the first time. I don't want to be jaded. I still want to have some of that innocence and fan's perspective even while I try to be an even-keeled broadcaster.

I don't know Aaron Rodgers personally, but I've certainly been impressed with how he handled the awkward time of transition as Packers fans dealt with the departure of Brett Favre. I never understood why Rodgers was the "bad guy" in some people's minds. I can remember going to practice the day that Favre was in Green Bay and eventually left to be traded to the Jets. There were fans with signs and boos for Rodgers. Those were totally uncalled for. You can love Brett Favre, but that's no reason to hate Aaron Rodgers. He is a rising star and the Packers are fortunate to have him.

Packers fans are truly unique. I've seen them in stadiums across the country display their loyalty and enthusiasm. I've seen them arrive at Lambeau Field at 8 am for a noon game and snap pictures in front of Lambeau Field as if it were a religious shrine. Maybe more than anything, I remember how they lined Oneida Street in the freezing cold for the victory motorcade that took forever after Super Bowl XXXI. In most places, there would have been a riot from impatience and frustration. But as we broadcast that parade and rally on television, all of the video showed fans who were so happy that they couldn't care less about the cold.

As great as it was to cover the Super Bowl victory in New Orleans, in many ways the NFC Championship game victory over Carolina was more fun because it came at Lambeau Field. The home fans had a chance to enjoy the accomplishment. I remember being on the field for the trophy presentation and just looking around Lambeau and soaking in the moment. Bob Harlan, Ron Wolf and Mike Holmgren made a magnificent organizational team and deserved their spots on the podium.

I've had a chance to see up-close the highs and lows. The Packers last game at County Stadium was an emotional day. I was just feet away from the end zone when Brett Favre leaped in. For a kid who grew up close to Milwaukee, it was sad to see that chapter of Packers history end. I was also on the sideline for the final seconds in that playoff game in San Francisco after the 1998 season. I was right by the end zone where Terrell Owens made that catch that knocked the Packers out of the playoffs and ended the Mike Holmgren era.

One of my favorite moments covering the Packers came on December 24th, 1995. The Packers clinched their first division title since 1972 with a dramatic home victory over Pittsburgh. Yancy Thigpen dropped a potential game-winning touchdown for the Steelers. We did a live postgame show on WTMJ-TV and LeRoy Butler was so happy that he kissed me on the cheek during an interview. I don't think I've ever been kissed by anyone else on live television. Although LeRoy remains one of my all-time favorites, I'm not sure he would have been my first choice for that distinction!

I often think, "What are the odds that a kid from Hartford who used to announce to himself in the driveway would get paid to do it as an adult?"

I've been lucky and blessed.

By Dennis Krause, Time Warner Sports 32

CR SO

17 Duane's Got Reggie's Back

The "man" who came to town in '94 was known best by just a first name, like Elvis. Called simply "Reggie," he was also known as the "Minister of Defense" because of his deep Christian faith and his ability to create havoc by sacking quarterbacks. In each of my two meetings with him, I came away with a sense of awe. The first meeting was at a training camp. Like many die-hards, I was there to see the Pack. I brought along my daughter, who stole the show that day.

It happened before the "circus" was in full bloom, as Packer camps would go. Reggie sauntered across the lot from Lambeau to the field. Like sharks pursuing a chum line, suddenly he was engulfed by 20, 30, possibly 50 people. I'm still not sure how many there actually were, but it was a massive group of all sizes and ages, each there to say hi and hopefully get his autograph, including my daughter Nicole.

"Daddy, can you get me Reggie's autograph?" she pleaded.

I looked into Nicole's eyes and then over at the mob swarming around Reggie.

"Honey, he's really busy right now. And look at the tons of people around him. I think it'll be nearly impossible to get close enough to him."

She would hear none of it. Clearly, I wasn't convincing her. So, I decided to take a chance for my little girl. I took off my Packer tiger striped hat (which I'd earned with fill-ups of gas for my car) and gave it to her along with my trusty black marker and some challenging instructions.

"If you can get it, you can have the cap and his autograph."

Off she went. Quickly disappearing into that mass of humanity was a little girl, my hat, and my pen, leaving me alone with my fears. I circled the group. I looked high and low, but I couldn't see her. Then I caught the motion of the big man's arm moving upward. My daughter had burrowed an alley through the crowd like Moses parting the Red Sea. She had found her target!

There she was, hat in hand and marker stretched up to her hero. The gracious giant looked down at me with a broad grin that confirmed he knew I was the brains behind sending the tyke to him rather than going myself.

"Hey, that was pretty good," he joked to me.

He signed the hat and also included his customary I Corinthians 13 on it. With one stealth maneuver that belied his huge size, she was back in my arms. She still beams from ear to ear when she recalls that day, and she still has the hat to show for it.

My second encounter with Reggie was at my job at JJ Keller in Neenah, and it was equally as memorable. Reggie and his wife, Sara, had come to speak and hand out awards during our company contest program.

This time I was on stage right next to him. I stood there like a star struck child. I didn't say a word. Then his wonderfully deep yet gentle voice broke into my stupor and he looked over to me.

"Hey, you're about as tall as I am?"

"Yeah, and I've got the bad back problems like you to match."

"You pray for my back and I'll pray for yours."

"Deal," I told him.

I did pray for Reggie often. I don't doubt that he kept his word and prayed for me, as well.

Those two great moments in my life were gifts from God that allowed me to meet the giant of a man I so deeply respected. What great gifts they were. And what a gift he was to all of us.

Thanks for the memories #92.

By Duane Wiedmeyer

CR SO

18 The Startled Muscatine

Believe it, or not, there are actually a few places in the world where there are no professional sports teams, including an NFL football team, for whom folks can cheer. Consequently, there are very few people in the world who are oblivious to pro sports, bringing us Karen Harkness.

Her hometown, Muscatine, IA, is one of those places where there are no hometown pro teams. Not surprising, then, that Karen had no allegiance to any particular team. Except for watching a couple of high school games, the only thing that came close to watching pro ball was when she attended an Iowa vs. Purdue Big Ten college football game, and her attendance at that was only to watch the cheerleaders perform.

Karen and her husband, Jody, arrived in Wisconsin in 1991 after he had been transferred from his job in Cedar Rapids, where he had been born and raised. Karen admits she knew very little about football. Jody, equally as honest, admits he wouldn't call himself a football fan either.

So, what did they know, particularly about the Green Bay Packers?

"I knew their uniforms were green and gold," she smiled.

Some would say that's pretty lame, but it's a start. Shortly after her arrival in the land of Lambeau, Karen had an awakening, of sorts, on a cold Wisconsin afternoon while placing a jar of apple sauce into her cart at Copps grocery.

"Not knowing the layout of the store, I went up and down each aisle very methodically," she recalls.

"I couldn't help but notice that the store was virtually empty of customers and it was incredibly quiet, except that I could hear a radio in the background. It wasn't the usual grocery store type of music, but I really wasn't listening too closely," she recalls.

"Suddenly, people are yelling and hollering. Their voices were getting louder and louder. It startled me. I confess I was actually a bit frightened. Had there been a robbery, or a medical emergency?" wondered the bewildered Iowan.

Her fear quickly turned to confusion as she turned the corner into the next aisle to discover both shoppers and employees alike now cheering and clapping.

"What happened?" she asked a woman standing on the edge of the gathering.

"The Packers just scored a go-ahead touchdown!" she gleefully replied, still listening to Packer announcer Jim Irwin give details of the play.

"Oh," she commented, a bit relieved.

"Honestly, I wanted to roll my eyes. All I could think was, 'Where have we moved our family to?'" Karen recounts, now clearly amused by the whole incident.

Obviously, it didn't take long for Karen to realize that the Packers rule in Wisconsin.

"Clearly, this community loves their football and they love their Packers," comments Karen 19 years after that startling day at Copps Food Store.

"The team is a big part of the social, cultural and economic engine that drives Wisconsin. The Packers are a legacy and a very family-friendly tradition."

What is the most redeemable thing about the team that Karen would tell others who are ready to move into the area?

"The team, the town and the organization are very community-minded and philanthropic. It's more than just a game. It's about taking care of each other here."

If you've just moved to Wisconsin, or you're making plans to do so, and you've never heard of the Green Bay Packers, don't get too rattled if you hear an uproar in the aisle of the grocery store on a Sunday afternoon.

By Steve Rose with memories from Karen Harkness

ଓ ଛ

19 Garett & the Green and Gold Teddy Bears

Childhood cancer. The mere mention of those two words can strike terror in the most stalwart of hearts, but what we have learned has been so valuable for us. Like so many in the Green Bay community whose families have been stricken by cancer, we have been the benefactors of the love and generosity of the Green Bay Packers.

Our youngest child, Garett, was diagnosed with Wilms Tumor at the tender age of nine and one-half months in August, 2005. What was devastating in one regard became, in another, an amazing time for our family. Our family believes in prayer, a lot! Prayer gave us the strength and confidence to move forward toward healing. That confidence grew when Garett's nurse, Nicole (Toonen) Schmeichel, approached us in the wee hours of the morning.

"Paul and Jacque, can I talk to you?"

"Of course," we assured her.

This would be the first of many blessings to follow.

"I, myself, am a survivor of a Wilms tumor."

You can only imagine how we felt! We bombarded her with questions and she patiently answered each and every one of them. It was difficult to wrap our brains around the idea of our baby having a kidney removed and going through chemotherapy for the next five months. It never occurred to us that our lives were going to be touched by so many people from all walks of life, nor could we imagine the blessings we would receive for years to come.

When our child was diagnosed with cancer, we discovered very quickly how everything in our lives would change. We'd miss things like parents' night out, hockey games, Christmas parties and other gatherings because Garett was so ill that first year after his diagnosis.

In 2006, we were finally able to attend our first family event in over a year. What a memorable one it was, a Christmas party with some Green Bay Packers, hosted by St. Mark Evangelical Lutheran Church in West De Pere. We had no idea what to expect. There was a clown making balloon animals, lots of games going on, and plenty of pizza & ice cream for everyone. The room was full of families, all of whom shared a powerful common bond.

The real commotion started when the jersey-clad Packers arrived. Suddenly, we were standing in the same room with Al Harris, Korey Hall, Mason Crosby and others. They came into the church without any fanfare and quietly began to approach the kids. To our amazement, they knew the names of the children and their parents. We were all deeply touched. The smiles and giggles from those kids were music to all of our ears. It was priceless to watch as these gentle, giant teddy bears sat down with the kids to sing Christmas songs together.

Garett, only two years old at the time, didn't know who the Packers were, but that didn't matter to them. We watched these big, grown men's tender hearts melt right before our eyes as they got down on the ground to play with the children. Parents took pictures while the Packers signed hats, shirts, or whatever the kids wanted them to sign.

"Say, could we have a picture taken with you and our son Garett?" we asked, approaching a few of the players.

It was an amazing time for all of us.

Those pictures serve as a reminder of just how special the Packers are, and continue to be, to the Green Bay community. We look at the players differently since then. We have always been, and will always be, Packer fans, but now our family has a special connection to the Packers that can never be broken.

To every player who will read this book, "Thank you for caring about us and our children. Thanks for taking the time to give a special memory to us and our children. Thanks for being who you are!"

As for our family, we now are more convinced than ever, as one Packer author once wrote, "God truly is a Packer Fan!"

By Jacque Wilson

CR ℘

Aaron Kampman holding Garett Wilson

20 Alyssa's 87 Smiles

Mom and Dad picked me up from school on the afternoon of September 16, 1996. I was eight years old. They told me we were going to do something fun that night. I had no clue as to what was going on, but I was beyond excited. We drove for a while before stopping at a McDonalds to get some supper. Dad leaned over his burger to ask me a question.

"Any idea where we're going?" he grinned mischievously.

"No." I said, grinning right back at him. They had always done such a good job of surprising me in the past.

When we got back into the car, Dad instructed me to put on my #87 Packer jersey. Suddenly, I got butterflies in my tummy. We drove for a little while longer and finally came to a stop in a parking ramp. As we got out of the car, Mom and Dad revealed the surprise, or at least part of it. We were going to a Packer book signing of a friend, and that's why we were dressed in our Packer gear.

The Retlaw Ballroom in Fond du Lac was huge to my eight-year-old sensibilities, and incredibly crowded. The entire room was lined with Packer memorabilia and Packer merchandise, including a lawn mower that had the Packer colors and the "G" symbol on it. Mom sat me on the lawn mower and took my picture. We watched the festivities going on all around us and talked with other Packer fans, especially those from our hometown of Campbellsport, WI.

My parents were constantly monitoring my expression. My smile just got broader and broader, but I was having a hard time seeing anything, so my dad lifted me up on his shoulders.

"Can you see up there, Lyss?"

"Uh-huh. I can now, Dad!" I squealed with delight.

Toward the front of the room I could see a couple of people making their way to the table. Suddenly, my heart started beating uncontrollably. I couldn't believe my eyes! There he was – my favorite Green Bay Packer ever, Robert Brooks!

Mom and Dad had taken me to a signing for Steve Rose's book, *Leap of Faith: God Must Be a Packer Fan*. Steve, who had gone to high school with my parents, had brought Robert with him for the book signing. Robert wore #87 while with the Packers, and was on the front cover of the book doing the "Lambeau Leap" he had made famous in the mid '90s during those Super Bowl years.

About an hour into the signing, Steve came up to my parents and asked us to follow him. Could it be? Yes! We were in line to get Robert Brooks' autograph. I was going to be up close to my favorite Packer player ever. I was so nervous when Steve finally introduced me to my hero.

"Alyssa, this is Robert Brooks."

"Hi," was all I could muster. I just looked up at him and smiled.

"Hi, Alyssa," he said to me with a broad smile across his face.

He was introduced to my parents, and then he signed a picture of himself that my parents had framed. Next, Steve took us to a secluded area where we had our picture taken with him, the same one that is on the cover of this book! We loved it so much that we used it as our Christmas card that year.

On our way home, I realized my face actually hurt from smiling so broadly for so long a period of time. I was so excited that I not only had met my Packer hero, but I actually had my picture taken with him. I will never forget the night! Our conversation with Robert wasn't long, but it meant the world to me and to my family. I don't know why, at the tender age of 8, I was so intrigued and captivated by Robert. Maybe it was his amazing talent on the field, or his seemingly kind demeanor off the field, or just his heartwarming smile. What I do know, however, is that I was definitely in Packer heaven that night!

I know that evening meant a lot to my dad, too, who's the biggest Packer fan in Campbellsport. Mom and Dad even have license plates that say PKRFN1 (Packer Fan #1).

Who would have thought that, fourteen years after that event, my family and I would be on the front cover of this book? I'm hoping for one more chance to meet my hero. If dreams do come true, maybe he'll sign my copy of this book. What a wonderful irony and reunion that would be.

I know it would bring back some warm and wonderful memories of an eight-year-old on her daddy's shoulders who got to meet her favorite Packer!

By Alyssa McGray

CR SO

21 From Lee to Lambeau

There are some clear indications that let you know the seasons have changed in Wisconsin. Frozen ground means that the leaves have been raked and cold winter weather has set in for awhile. Warmer air and wet streets from mounds of melting snow are hopeful signs of an impending spring, leading to a hot summer. The sound of Wayne Larrivee's incredibly passionate voice on most fall-winter Sundays means only one thing, Packer season.

Lee, a town in the western part of Massachusetts, is a stone's throw from the New York border. It's from that vantage point that Wayne Larrivee, the radio voice of the Packers since 1999, watched the Packers. Well, actually there were a few times he was out-in-the-cold listening to them because Green Bay games were not prominent on TV during the '60s when he became a Packer fan.

"Most of the time we got the Giants on CBS, sometimes the Packers and the Colts, or the Packers and 49ers," remembers Wayne. "I thought the 'G' on the helmet was so unique, so I gravitated to them."

He remembers one quarterback and a certain situation that happened often.

"It would be 3rd and 1. Rather than run the ball, Bart Starr would call a pass to Boyd Dowler or Carroll Dale for 15 yards. Those were some of my earlier memories."

Wayne vividly recalls his school lunch box that had #31 on it. He loved watching Jim Taylor who wore that number. He can still see Paul Hornung being led by Jerry Kramer and Fuzzy Thurston on a power sweep. He remembers nearly freezing to death while listening to a game that would become one of the most significant games ever played in NFL or sports history.

"My dad was a ski patrolman. He got paid by getting ski passes for our family. We skied in the mornings on Friday, Saturday and Sunday, no exception," recalls Wayne.

On Sunday, December 31, 1967, the 11-yr-old asked his father if he could take a timeout from the slopes. There was no TV in the Ski Lodge, so he had to call an audible, if you will.

"Dad, can I listen to the Packers play the Cowboys in the NFL Championship game today?"

"Okay," he dad acquiesced, albeit reluctantly.

"So I got into the Red Mercury to listen to Van Patrick. It was cold, and the car barely started, but I'll never forget that game or that day. It was pretty cold where I was, but not nearly as cold as it was in Green Bay."

So when did the broadcast bug bite Wayne?

"I was a sophomore in high school when I realized that I wasn't going to play sports, but I loved to follow the game. I went to Emerson College and graduated with a degree in Mass Communications. Then I got a job in Davenport, Iowa, where I did play-by-play for the Iowa Hawkeyes."

But it was the professional games that the gifted Larrivee had his sights set on. In 1978, he sent a tape to KCMO in Kansas City and before long he was doing the Kansas City Chiefs, which led to the Chicago Bears for 14 years while also doing work in the Windy City for the Bulls. ESPN Regional, NCAA Basketball on the Big Ten Network and Westwood One got added to his repertoire, but the best gig was just around the corner.

"Because of my time with the Bears, I got to know the voice of the Packers, Jim Irwin, and he shared with me that he was going to be retiring. So, in 1999, Paul LeSage from WTMJ gave me a shot, and here I am today. This is a dream job," says a grateful Larrivee.

He remembers his Packer beginnings very well.

"The first game was a preseason game against the Chiefs at Lambeau and the first regular season game was against the Oakland Raiders, which we won at the end. It was significant because it was Ray Rhodes' first game."

Wayne, a proud dad, had his son Bryan working with him as his spotter in the booth on game days for 10 years. His older son, Scott, who was attending the University of Wisconsin, was also able to attend a number of Packers games, including the first regular season game Wayne broadcast for the Packers, the opener in 1999, a thrilling last-second victory over the Raiders in Lambeau Field.

"I remember coming down the elevator from the broadcast booth on the first day when Scott said, 'Dad, this is what we came here for.' That was a special moment."

If there is a more excitable or more passionate play-by-play guy in the world, I haven't heard him. Wayne gave some insight as to where that passion originates.

"I believe every play has a passion about it. I try to give every play its just due. I believe local announcers should be upset if things aren't going well. If the Packers make a great play, that should be obvious in the voice inflection, as well," he suggests.

Wayne has nothing but high praise for his broadcast partner, Larry McCarren (the Packer Rock). When asked to point out a few of the players that have impressed him off-the-field, he's quick to bring up two.

"Aaron Kampman is one of the finest people I've met in my thirty-some years of covering NFL teams. Aaron does tremendous good deeds borne of desire, not duty. We'll miss him in Green Bay in every way." (See also: Wise in His Goings)

"Then there's the other Aaron. I had no doubt he'd become a great quarterback in the league. Rodgers' first collegiate start was California at Illinois, and I had the joy of calling that game."

While the crowd in the Lambeau Atrium groaned in '05 upon hearing Rodgers fell in the draft, Wayne actually got excited.

"I told people that Ted Thompson had made a great pick for down the road."

The rest of that story speaks for itself, and clearly points to the Larrivee's acumen to spot talent.

I personally love Wayne's exclamation point to Packer wins, particularly after a big play that puts the game out of reach for the opponents.

"And there is your dagger!" he will roar.

This 'catch phrase' has become synonymous with Larrivee and it is believed that he's the announcer that led a surge of other announcers to use the phrase, as well.

Wayne Larrivee is one of the leaders in his field. No one would argue that he has the best gig in the business. Just think. It all began when he saw that 'G' on the helmet, and carried a Jimmy Taylor #31 lunch box on his way to Lambeau, via Lee, Massachusetts.

By Steve Rose with memories from Wayne Larrivee

CR ☙

22 A Class Act

For many, Bob Harlan represents the heart and soul of the greatest professional sports franchise in the world, the Green Bay Packers. I understand that. Anyone's who's been fortunate enough to meet and talk with him will tell you that Bob may be one the nicest men in the world, no exaggeration.

I've had the pleasure of spending time with Bob Harlan on three separate occasions. Bob was gracious enough to take my phone call when I wanted to interview him for our first project, *Leap of Faith: God Must Be a Packer Fan.*

Even before then, however, I had heard the stories of how he answered his own phone, simply because he felt that it was his responsibility to do so. I thought that may have been one of many tall tales that come out of "Titletown" until one day I nervously picked up the phone and dialed a number I had been told was his direct line.

"Hello, this is Bob Harlan."

I'm seldom if ever at a loss for words, but it took me a second or two to get my bearings. He really does answer his own phone!

"Mr. Harlan, my name is Steve Rose…and I'm uhh…"

"Steve, first of all, please call me Bob," he insisted.

"Okay, uhh, Bob. I'm writing a Packer book and I was wondering if I could ask you a few questions?"

"Sure, how can I help you, Steve?"

Bob was incredibly gracious in giving me the time necessary to ask my questions, and equally generous in answering them. Since then, I've been one of the biggest boosters in the "Robert E. Harlan Fan Club." Time is such a valuable commodity for most people and I've learned to respect others' time when seeking their assistance in order to do my own job.

I caught up with Bob in early October 2009 and again during the writing of this book. We were heading up the elevator to get 60 minutes of video footage in Bob's office. He loves to talk about the Green Bay Packers! At that time I had a very specific question on my mind. I hoped that in answering it, perhaps he would be able to bare what I suspected may be a very heavy heart. It was only a few days after the first Packer-Viking game with, uh, that #4 guy playing in purple.

"Bob, can I ask your feelings about the game the other night?"

"Honestly, Steve, I was so torn I couldn't watch it."

It is understandable that with Bob's deep love for the Green Bay Packers and the respect and admiration he held for Brett Favre that Bob would be conflicted on the subject.

"Madeline and I were watching a movie and I said, 'Oh just turn it on to see what the score is.'"

That may not have been the best idea.

"She hit the remote at the exact moment that Rodgers got hit and fumbled," he paused. "We turned the radio on the next morning and heard the score."

Bob was clearly grieved, but he finished his thoughts.

"And when they (Vikings) come to Green Bay, I won't watch that game either."

In retrospect, that was a good decision.

Working with the Packers organization has been the greatest experience for Bob. I asked what his managing philosophy was.

"Hire good people, tell them what you want them to do, and then get out of their way," he finished.

It's a good philosophy, which led to hiring Ron Wolf, who hired Mike Holmgren, who would coach a quarterback Wolf traded for in 1991.

Speaking of Wolf, Bob told me a funny story.

"We were playing the Lions at Lambeau in December. It was cold. We were holding Barry Sanders' yards down pretty well when Ron looked over at me with a smile."

"Bob, should we turn the warming coils off at halftime?" he questioned.

With the coils turned off, the field would have truly become the frozen tundra, a virtual ice rink. Wolf was kidding. At least Bob believes that he was!

Bob Harlan continues to serve in a powerful public capacity after having given the reins to Mike Murphy in 2007. His shining moment and finest work may have been when he literally went out and shook hands with the public in the beginning of the new decade to gain support for the Brown County tax legislation needed to help pay for the $295 million renovation of Lambeau Field. That renovation would make it possible for the Packers to continue in Green Bay.

Radio investor, entrepreneur and former Packer Hall of Fame Board member Jim Coursolle got to know Bob well. I mentioned to Jim that the $295 million dollar renovation saved the Packers hundreds of millions of dollars because, had they waited two to three years more, the cost would have gone to $750 million.

"No, Steve, Bob Harlan didn't just save them some money. He actually saved the Packers!"

"What?"

"Bob Harlan 'saved' the Packers."

One of the nicest men you'll ever meet may very well be the one to thank for the privilege of watching the Packers wear the green-and-gold at home in the very place to which they belong, Green Bay, WI.

Thanks Bob.

By Steve Rose with memories from Bob Harlan

CR SO

23 Noah Docks in Green Bay

It's so refreshing, and rather unusual, to find any young man who has his priorities in order. It may be an ever greater challenge to keep them in order if you've had the opportunity to spend time in Green Bay with the Packers. Noah Herron's helmet hung in the locker room at 1265 Lombardi Avenue in Green Bay from 2005 to 2006 until an injury ended his memorable journey there. He still calls Green Bay home even though he's since had stints in the NFL with Tampa Bay and Cleveland. By the way, he arrived in Green Bay via the Pittsburgh Steelers in '05 after being drafted out of the Big Ten's Northwestern as a running back.

I met this chiseled 5'11" 215-lb young man at a Chili's restaurant for lunch, and in the course of our conversation together learned that there were a couple of really good reasons why he was spending time in

Appleton at the writing of this story. First, he was rehabbing a shoulder that was nearly five months out from surgery and, second, he loves the Fox River Valley area that encompasses the Wisconsin cities of Green Bay, Appleton, Neenah-Menasha and several other smaller cities and communities.

"So, Noah, where'd ya grow up?" I quizzed him.

"I was born in Milwaukee and moved to Mattawan, MI, at four. It is a community of about 2,400 people. I graduated in 2000 from Mattawan High School. Funny thing was, I was a huge Barry Sanders fan, not so much a Lions fans, but I hated Brett Favre," he grinned coyly. "And I told him too."

I had a feeling I knew where this was going.

"Before I got drafted, I have to admit that Green Bay was #32 (last) on the list of teams that I wanted to play for, and I told Brett that as soon as I met him. I'd tell him that all the time. He'd just shake his head and laugh."

He eventually became a good friend of Brett and Deanna, and the friendship continues to this day.

"We used to have dinner every Tuesday night either at my place or theirs. When I was training in Louisiana, Brett and Deanna would invite me to come over to their place in Hattiesburg. I was more than happy to make the couple-hour trip 'cuz we always had such a great time and we became strong friends."

I asked him if there were others he came to know and appreciate during his time in Green Bay. He mentioned that Samkon Gado was a good friend and fellow Christian. One other former Packer player, and current coach, got some pretty healthy praise from Herron.

"Edgar Bennett is a great person and solid role model. I stay in contact with him to this day."

He stopped just long enough to wolf down a few chips and salsa before continuing.

"This organization is great from top to bottom. From the people in the front office, Mr. Murphy, to Red Batty, Jeff Blumb, Sherry Shuldes, Doug Collins, they're all great human beings. It's not like that in other towns or with other teams."

Pretty kind words coming from a kid who admits he "hated" Brett Favre just a few years prior.

"So, Noah, do you think people take less money just to stay here?" I quizzed again.

"I think they might if they're here already. I think it's a possibility. There's some culture shock at first. I mean, you can only go downtown, or to the mall so many times before you realize you've exhausted all your options. By then though you've realized how nice the people are, and then you begin to appreciate even more the special tradition of this team, and the town, and you don't want to leave," he smiled.

My hope for Noah is that by the time you read this, he's been picked up by another NFL team. He did mention that there's one team who may be interested in him.

"You know, if God wants me playing in the NFL, I just need to do my part and work hard, and it will all work out. I've been blessed to make some money in this profession, but if I need to go to the next phase of my life, and it doesn't include football, I'm okay with that."

On the way to our cars we exchanged a hug and I encouraged him to remember this small word of wisdom.

"You'll have options, my friend. You will have options!"

"Hey, thanks. I appreciate that."

I admire anyone who has the looks, the personality, the talent and the gifting that this 28-year-old has, and can still have his priorities in order. That, to me, speaks loudly of his true character and I for one am glad that for a season, well, two Noah docked in Green Bay.

By Steve Rose with help from Noah Herron

CR &D

24 Willie Wood Could and Did

I remember watching Willie Wood play in the defensive backfield for the Green Bay Packers on the glory day teams, and in both Super Bowls I & II. I especially recall a picture in a magazine of Willie in uniform, jumping up to touch the cross bar on a football goal post. That may not seem like a big feat, but Willie was only 5' 10." The man had springs in his legs!

William Vernell Wood Sr. was born in 1936 in Washington, DC. He loved to play football and had the pleasure of playing with the USC Trojans, but the best was yet to come, even after a bit of a setback. Willie was not drafted by an NFL team, but he was given a tryout by the Packers in 1960. They liked what they saw, and he was signed. Willie played free safety and he was a starter right up until his retirement in 1971.

Wood won numerous honors throughout his career. He is in the Pro Football Hall of Fame, but that and other accomplishments are not as important as the relationships he built and the memories he carries with him today.

His son, Willie Wood Jr., tells us how his dad, recently diagnosed with demential, is doing these days.

"Most days he's himself, telling jokes and stories. It's been a decade since he's been in Green Bay, but he still loves to talk about the Glory Days."

Here's what the elder Wood had to say about that.

"Both Vince Lombardi and my teammates have had a major effect on my life. Those Lombardi years were great. Coach had such a positive influence in my life as a player and business person."

"There never has been, nor will there ever be, a place like Green Bay. I was never just a guy in town on the team. I always felt like I was from there. Green Bay doesn't simply have fans, they were and are our teammates. The Packers get woven into the fabric of the community, and the community gets woven into the fabric of the team," he said confidently.

Wood's immediate circle of friends always included Bob Jeter and Herb Adderly, with whom he still keeps in touch today. Jerry Kramer has always been a dear friend of Willie and the family, as well.

What are Willie Jr's recollections of living in Green Bay?

"I don't remember much because I was young, but I do remember that it was cold!" he laughs. "I've never met anyone from Green Bay that I didn't like. It's special to be a fan. It's like being born with freckles," he points out. "I grew up with the Packers in my DNA."

The Woods both agreed they wanted to share this one last thought with all the die-hard fans.

"We are each men, fathers and Packer fans. You can pick the order!" joked Willie Jr.

Woods Sr. currently lives in Washington, D.C., in an assisted-care facility. Although his physical heart is living close to the White House, Willie's Packer heart will always be at Lambeau Field.

By Steve Rose with memories from Willie Wood Jr. and Sr.

ଓ ଞ

25 Dorsey's $2500 Pants

It was 1997. I was moving a Packer to his new home. While unloading the truck and bringing in furniture, it was hard not to notice that one of the neighbors, who was on his riding mower, was going back and forth continuously, his eyes more on us than his lawn. Then I saw that a group of neighbors across the street had gathered together to watch us. Finally, I realized they weren't watching us, they were watching their new neighbor, running back Dorsey Levens.

I couldn't help but laugh as I was making my next trip into the house.

"Say, Dorsey. If you want to meet your new neighbors, this might be a good opportunity. And you might end up saving the guy on the lawn mower from running into a tree," I joked.

He smiled, went out, and took a few minutes to meet them. Later, I came into the kitchen to find Dorsey cleaning and putting things away. He had a green and gold pile of something on the table.

"What's that?" I asked.

"It's the game pants I was wearing when I broke the single season Packer rushing record," he told me, holding them up for me to see.

"Can you use 'em for one of your charities?" he asked.

"Heck, yeah!" I answered. With one short flick of the wrist, he tossed them to me.

I tossed them right back at him, much to his apparent surprise.

"What?" he quizzed.

"Ya gotta sign them!" I explained. "Then they'll be worth good money."

He grabbed a big black marker from the counter and signed them. Now, right along with the dirt, the blood, and the grass stains, was Dorsey Levens' signature. My buddy made a great big frame for them and we auctioned them off that year for Children's Hospital of Wisconsin. My brother-in-law, Joel Hinze had the winning bid of $1,000.

The best and rest of the story happened the following year. Joel donated them back to Children's Hospital to be auctioned off again. This time they garnered $1,500!

Do the math with me. Those pants added $2,500 to the coffers of the Children's Hospital of Wisconsin. And you thought Dorsey Levens was just a great running back! I can say from experience he's an even better person, and a wonderfully generous one at that.

By Gary Long

 (3 80)

26 #26 Taught Me How to Play

I grew up near Ripon, WI. located an hour north of Milwaukee. Let me mention that I love music, and play numerous instruments. I believe in doing everything the best that it can be done. It was that same attitude in Chuck Cecil that drew me to him. The ferocious heat-seeking, hard-hitting missile was a part of the 1989 "Heart attack Pack." That's when I became a true Packer fan. Cecil, #26, played for Green Bay from 1988 to 1992.

My man, Chuck, may have been an undersized safety at 6'0" and 185 lbs., but his size could not diminish his enthusiasm for whatever he undertook. Growing up, I wanted to play music as well as Chuck played football, and I pledged that I would give it my all. My family would just cringe with excitement when Chuck would 'lay the wood' to an opposing receiver coming across his territory in the defensive backfield. As I remember it, they often cringed when I hit a wrong note on my trumpet, too. I was not deterred. I kept on "hitting it hard" and practicing, just like Chuck.

If you're too young to know who I'm talking about, Chuck was the guy with the great smile who had a constant cut over the bridge of his nose from hitting receivers so hard. He always looked like someone had taken a ketchup bottle and poured it over his nose each week. He became so well known for his tough-guy look that people in the stands started putting red stuff over the bridges of their noses to be like Chuck.

Chuck was a great player, no doubt about it, but I learned something even more valuable from him in my junior year of high school. While doing research for a paper on Chuck, I learned he had a 3.85 grade-point average through high school. He was never offered a scholarship to play football, so he had to be a "walk on" at the University of Arizona, meaning he was invited to try to make the team, but there would be no offer of financial assistance. My family and I admired his hard work ethic and blue-collar attitude.

By the way, I did play football as a receiver in high school. Today I play music with our band, Copper Box. I give it everything I have on every note, every gig, just like Chuck taught me to.

Someday I hope to meet him and thank him personally. My wife, Michelle, and I are raising our children with that same kind of passion I saw in Chuck. Our hope is that whatever they choose to do, they'll do it with everything they have, just like good old #26, Chuck Cecil did.

By Danny Jerabek

CR ЮD

27 Freedom Isn't Free

When my friend, Heather Coonen, called to invite me to the Packers vs. Ravens game in 2009, I was elated. It had been over a year since I last attended a game and I missed the atmosphere and vibe that came with going to a game. This particular game fell on December 7. It was a cold Monday night, so I dressed in four different layers to combat the frigid temperatures

When we arrived at our seats, I complimented Heather on her season tickets. They were fabulous. We were 12 rows up in the end zone, right above the "Lambeau Leap" section. As I peered out over the field, I could hear and see every detail with stunning perfection. The anticipation on the players' faces, the intricate sewing on the colorful uniforms, and each crunch of the turf brought a whole new meaning to the word "awesome." It was, indeed, a little slice of heaven, until I heard …them.

Sitting in front of us were three men with really heavy Jersey accents. Their accents were so thick I could barely understand one word, much less understand their obnoxious chants. All I could envision was these three yo-yos babbling through the entire game and ruining it for all of us who were seated around them. I simply couldn't let it happen.

Anyone who knows me well will acknowledge that I'm not one to back down from confrontation. In fact, sometimes I actually get a natural high from the adrenaline rush a good tongue lashing can give. As a woman of girth and stature, I can command respect, and I was going to get it. So, with my mouth loaded, I gently tapped each one on the shoulder.

"Hey, guys. Your chants aren't welcome here, okay?"

I stood firm, fully anticipating a verbal assault, but it never came. What I received, instead, has remained stuck in my head every day since.

The one in the middle spoke first.

"Ma'am, I apologize."

Then a second fellow spoke up, and his response was sobering to both me and my friends.

"My son has just come home from his second tour in Iraq," he began. "I promised him, when he arrived home, that I'd take him and his brother to as many professional football games as we could fit in during his leave."

The father of these two young men went on to tell us they had already been to New York, Pittsburgh, Minnesota, Chicago, and the last stop, his favorite, to Green Bay. He then apologized again, and offered to buy us all a round of beer.

I stood on the cold concrete floor, my mouth open so wide I could have caught a touchdown pass in it. My heart sank and I was completely embarrassed. How could I have overlooked the soldier's slim build and crew cut? How could I not have known? My heart was heavy and tears rimmed my eyes. I knew I had to say something…again.

"I am so sorry for my response to you." My voice cracked as I apologized.

He graciously accepted it. I was humbled and brought back to earth. I became so grateful for this young man and his family and I wanted to tell everyone about it. This young service man put his life in danger so that you and I could enjoy this simple freedom in life, a Packer game.

After I apologized, all was forgiven. Together, my girls and the posse in front of us screamed the entire time, slapping high fives and booing bad calls. We ate, drank, and we were merry, as the Packers beat the Ravens 27-14.

At the end of the game we hugged, with genuine gusto, the men in front of us, and we vowed never to forget this simple lesson, that freedom is never free.

By Becky Herring

Heather Coonen, Meredith Sprovier, Dawn Brown, Rebecca Herring

ೞ ಜ

28 A Pint-Sized Packer Fan

Packer fans come in all shapes, sizes, and ages. Some of the most rabid fans are the ones of the female variety, as evidenced by one of the tiniest, and quite possibly one of the cutest, Packer fans ever. Nancy had given her niece, Lauren, a Packer jersey for her birthday. To be more specific, Nancy had given her a Brett Favre jersey, but it was a bit big for the then rambunctious two-year-old. By Christmas, 2009, however, little Lauren had grown into it, in more ways than one.

Now, we don't need to make unnecessary commentary here, but if you do the math and check the calendar, the odds of someone wearing a Green Bay Packer Favre jersey at that particular time in Packer history would have been minimal. There was one little girl, however, who could care less about Packer family controversy.

Below is an e-mail that Nancy got from Sheila, Lauren's mom, on January 14, 2009, thanking her for the Brett Favre jersey. You'll find it amusing unless, of course, you're Sheila.

Nancy,

I am so sick of the Brett Favre jersey I could scream – thanks a lot!!! Just Kidding! She honestly has worn it for about 2 weeks straight now. I won't let her wear it to daycare though (because it's dirty), so I have to deal with her temper tantrum every morning for about 15 minutes. The first thing she talks about, though, when I pick her up – "go home – put Brett Favre on." The first thing she told her teacher this morning was that "Brett Favre at home." She puts it on the minute we walk in the door, and insists on wearing it over her pajamas every night. I don't know what it is, but she is absolutely obsessed with it. I can't even get it off long enough to wash it – it has stains all over it right now! I wish Brett Favre would sign it – but we couldn't get it off long enough to send it to him! Now Scott bought her a little Nerf football and she has to carry that around with her – she is the strangest little girl ever!

Lauren Stettbacher

Love,
Sheila

If there's a moral to this story, perhaps it would be that the next time you want to get a little Packer fan a present, a doll or a baseball bat might be a wiser choice!

Steve Rose with e-mail from
Nancy Pfeifer

છ્ર જી

29 Little Mike McCoy

There have been two Mike McCoys to invade the hallowed ground of Lambeau Field, "Big Mike" and "Little Mike." Little Mike spent his entire career, which lasted from 1976 to 1983, wearing the green-and-gold. Born in 1953 in West Memphis, Arkansas, he was a Green Bay Packer fan since childhood, a clear indication, some might say, of his vast intelligence.

Little Mike grew up having it "tough." Perhaps that's what made him such a tough guy on the field, facing many opposing offensive lineman, including the physical (some called him dirty) Conrad Dobler of the Cardinals or Ram Jackie Slater. Little Mike never backed down. His nickname was the "Tasmanian Devil." Well, there was one time he did back down, but that one, in Mike's mind, doesn't really count.

With the 72nd pick of the 1976 NFL Draft, the Green Bay Packers selected Mike out of the University of Colorado-Boulder. After spending time watching primarily the Packers, Lions, Bears and occasionally the St. Louis Cardinals, one day Mike's dream to play in the NFL came true, and with a bonus.

"I was told that I was probably going to be picked by either the 49ers or the Raiders," remembers McCoy. "I was thrilled when I got a call from Bart Starr (head coach at the time) telling me I was going to be drafted by the Packers."

Dave Logan, who would also play in the NFL, had a warning for Mike.

"Man, you're goin' to the coldest place in the world," Logan teased his friend.

"I told him I didn't care. Those years turned out to be some of the greatest years of my life," Mike remembers fondly.

As for the numbers on the field, Mike had 13 interceptions, picked up five fumbles and rattled more than a few cages with the likes of teammates Willie Buchanon, Johnny Gray and Steve Luke in the defensive backfield. They were called the Swat Team because of their incredible abilities to knock away passes intended for receivers.

Little Mike acknowledges that he learned some great lessons from his teammates and from Coach Starr and a little something special from fellow DB Johnny Gray. He remembers Gray as a nasty hitter on the field, but a softhearted teddy bear off the field.

"I didn't know what community service was until I saw Johnny Gray," McCoy admitted. "He'd do autograph sessions with kids. I mean, he was right in the middle of them…right down in the dirt."

Although all turned out well for Little Mike in Green Bay, he did get off to a rough start, at least where Willie Buchanon and Buchanon's buddy were concerned.

"In 1976, I played in the last College All-Star game in Chicago. It kept me away from my rookie camp for about two weeks. Willie Buchanon was really riding me when I finally came in. I guess if he liked you, that's what he did to you. But after a while I got tired of it and him, really tired," McCoy recalls.

So, Little Mike came up with a plan.

"We were at St. Norbert College staying in the dorms as we always did in the pre-season and I was gonna call Buchanon 'out' to finally settle this whole thing. I was gonna get him off my back. And if I needed to rough him up a bit, I was considering it."

Little Mike waited, and waited. Willie never showed, but his bodyguard did.

"Well, out walks Dave Pureifory* who was a really big and strong defensive lineman for the Pack. He was also Willie's buddy. He'd do about 100-lb dumb bells in each hand. Looked like on this day, I was gonna be his dumb bell, I guess," laughed McCoy. "The other thing I didn't know was, while in school at Eastern Michigan, he was enrolled in the art of Jishukan-Ryu Jujitsu."

Arms folded across his massive chest, Dave had one question for the rookie.

"What's the problem?"

"Uh, nothing," he told Pureifory. "Not a thing."

"Willie and I never had a problem after that. We eventually became really good friends and still are to this day."

Although the sport is brutal, Mike, like many of the players, doesn't regret what it cost him to be able to play. Mike admits he was able to do more than make a good living for himself.

"I was able to buy my parents a home and take care of my siblings and for that I am so grateful. I would do the same thing over again. In order to get something in this life you have to sacrifice," remarked McCoy in

Mike McCoy and his wife Janet Brown

his soft and humble manner.

Little Mike is now 57 years old and has recently been diagnosed with dementia. While in Appleton in 2010 for a golf tournament to benefit the Children's Hospital of Wisconsin, he laughed with buddies Willie Buchanon, Johnny Gray and "Mac" Lane, who actually took on the role of caretaker, as well. MacArthur Lane had been told earlier by Janet Brown that Mike had to take some medication designed to help with dementia, but the meds had to be taken at a very specific time.

"Okay, that's no problem. I'll set the timer on my watch, and make sure he gets 'em," Mac graciously responded as they ambled down the fairway.

It seems that Little Mike is being taken care of pretty well these days, just like he took care of the Packer end zone at Lambeau from enemy invasion.

In Memorium to Dave Pureifory, July 12, 1949 – July 5, 2009

By Steve Rose with memories from "Little" Mike McCoy

CR ഗ്

30 Taking the Air Out of the Packers

In August 2000 and 2001, I had the pleasure of performing at the After Training Camp Packer Dinner held on the St. Norbert College campus. I was there primarily to entertain the children. What they didn't know was that I am fully capable of entertaining all ages. I was hired to do some tableside strolling entertainment (balloon animals and juggling), followed by a stage show.

I really wanted to engage not just the children, but the players as well, so I began the show with fire juggling. That always gets everyone's attention. Throughout my performances, I use volunteers, including children, who are in the audience. If a child volunteers, I make him a balloon animal as a gift. After I had done that a few times, I went over to a very large Packer player, who I believe was a defensive lineman, and challenged him to a duel.

"Hey, brother, who do you think can blow an animal balloon up faster, you or me?" I asked him.

Keep in mind that I'm 5'10" and weigh in at 160 pounds. My challenger was, shall we say, much, much bigger. The audience laughed and cheered and his friends egged him on. I grabbed a fresh balloon and gave it to my Packer helper. Then I got one for myself and stretched it a few times. My new Packer friend looked me square in the eye.

"You're 'toast,' buddy!" he joked.

I had the crowd do the countdown.

"On your mark, get set…go!"

I had my balloon inflated in not quite three seconds. My green-and-gold challenger, on the other hand, was huffing, puffing and really struggling. What a site to behold. His cheeks puffed way out and he turned bright red. The audience was loving it.

"Whoo hoo!" they shouted, cheering both of us on.

Finally finished, he spiked his balloon like Ryan Grant after a touchdown.

"You must have given me a bad one," was his excuse. "Give me a new one!"

With a shy, but knowing smile, I happily honored his request. I also took a new balloon for myself. We both melodramatically stretched our balloons, to the delight of the children. Again, the crowd gave the countdown. I inflated mine in about three seconds again. (What they forgot is that I am a professional, too.)

Once again he tried and, once again, he threw the balloon to the ground.

"Give me another one!"

Amid the raucous of cheering and laughing, we went through the same routine yet again, only this time my big Packer buddy called a friend up to try it along with him. Now his friends' cheeks puffed way out and he turned beet red. Another Packer player ventured forward to give it a try, but met with the same failing results as the prior players had.

"What's your trick?" they asked me, more than a little frustrated.

"Practice, practice, practice," I grinned.

What I most appreciated about these fellows was their willingness to help me entertain the crowd at the expense of looking foolish, and a bit like wimps. Although these guys hate to lose, they played along and were really good sports.

Hanging out with some Packer players and their families that night made for an event I'll never forget, but the best part for me is I can now say I beat up on a couple of Green Bay Packers.

By Dan Kirk, "Juggler with the Yellow Shoes"

ରେ ଛର

31 It Isn't Easy Being Green in Dallas

Being a Packer fan in Dallas was never an easy thing, much less in the '90s, when the Cowboys were peaking and everyone was jumping on the bandwagon (as Cowboy fans do). It was always great when the Packers would finally play the Cowboys so I could watch them on the local television station. There were several Packer bars in Dallas and, naturally, I had my own favorite. The comforting thing about watching the games there was that I always saw the same people every Sunday dressed in their green-and-gold finest, same as me. The cutest were the four and five-year-old little girls in Packer cheerleader outfits. There were also people in their 80s in wheelchairs who needed help getting through the door, but that never stopped them from being part of the gang.

We all got to know each other during the football season. We were all in the same difficult predicament, putting up with the same grief and merciless teasing from Cowboy fans. When the new season came around, it turned into a reunion of sorts, and the conversation and fellowship would pick up right where we had left it eight months earlier.

On January 14, 1995, I decided to venture out of my safe haven with a few friends to go to a local pub. I'm not sure what possessed me, but instead of going to my usual local haunt, I chose to head into the heart of Cowboy country, Randy White's Sports Bar and Grill, owned by legendary HOF Cowboy defenseman Randy White who, ironically, won the Lombardi Award in college. His place was known for big parties, especially during Cowboy games. To make my appearance memorable to all, I wore green and gold camouflage pants, a Packer jersey and, most notably, a Cheesehead hat, something I wouldn't normally wear.

Any Packer fan will tell you that it was very, very difficult when the Cowboys were on top of the NFL during the mid 90s, even though our Packers were on the rise. The Cowboys beat the Packers in the playoffs the previous two years, but we were getting better and it was only a matter of time before we would prevail.

Though there were only a few other Packer fans to be found, I entered with my head held high and a voice that boomed out a cheer for the Pack. That, of course, received an overwhelmingly critical response from the Cowboy fan base. No surprise there. I knew I was taking my life into my own hands. We managed to find a table, surrounded by my kind of Cowboy fans, people who wanted to give me a hard time, but did it all in good fun.

As the game went on, I had ample opportunity to jump up and make a scene, followed by several calls for me to shut up and sit down. In the end, the Packers lost 38-27.

What happened next was like something right out of a movie. First, the table next to mine bought me a condolence drink, sympathetic to the fact I was grieving the loss. They even acknowledged their appreciation for the loyalty displayed by Packer fans. Of course, they also mentioned I may have been a bit foolish for coming to Randy White's place.

Next, the entire staff came to my table and presented me with a piece of cheese cake as both a joke, and as a gesture of good will. I even let them throw a few Cowboy barbs at me. I ate the cheesecake, grinning from ear to ear.

I barely had finished shoveling the last bite of cake into my mouth when I looked up to see a mountain of a man hovering over me. Suddenly, former Cowboy, and owner of the place, Randy White, pulled out a large bowie knife, grabbed my cheesehead hat and cut it in half! You can imagine just how loudly the crowd roared. I admit, my stomach did a flip flop and, at that moment, I was wishing I hadn't eaten that cheese cake. Randy put his knife away, turned and walked away, only to return a few minutes later to make sure no one was giving me too hard of a time. Then, without my asking for it, he gave me his autograph.

When it was time to leave, I asked for my bill. I was told Randy had

Matt Struble and former Cowboy Randy White

taken care of it, suggestive of the possibility that even Cowboys and their fans can be nice once and awhile.

The next year the joke was on my Cowboy pals when we won the Super Bowl. That same year, I met a distant cousin in Dallas who, upon discovering I was a Packer fan, told me a story about some nut who went to Randy White's, kept the crowd riled up, and got his cheesehead hat cut in half by Randy. I just sat there with a big grin on my face. Funny how stories like that tend to spread so quickly.

A note to the wise, or to the not-so-wise, a proprietary word of caution. If you go to a certain food and drink place in Dallas, you may want to leave your cheesehead hat in the car!

By Matt Struble

CR ☙

32 Robbie Goes to Camp

One of the more admirable qualities of many of the Packer players is their generosity with their time, talents and resources. A fine example of this is that over the years Don Beebe, Robert Brooks and several other players have held football camps to share with up-and-coming athletes how to play the game, while also encouraging them to become better young men as they prepared for real life.

In 2004, Robbie Hummel had the opportunity to attend former Packer fullback William Henderson's Camp. Robbie's gifting and talent earned him the William Henderson award for all-around athlete and leadership at that camp. In 2006, he won the fullback award. Like many of the young men who have been fortunate enough to attend such camps, both the memories and the disciplines they were taught have carried over today.

One of those memorable moments came when Robbie's mom and dad, Trisha and Rob, came to the last day of camp to watch the games and the award ceremonies. Packer linebacker Nick Barnett, an easy going and good-natured fellow Packer, was helping out his teammate Will. As gracious as always, he extended his hand to the Hummels as they approached him.

"Hi, how are you?" he cordially asked.

"It's nice to meet you," said Trish and Rob, almost in unison.

They continued to exchange pleasantries when suddenly the topic of conversation shifted. Let's just say that Robbie has always looked a bit "beyond his years," and Nick was quick to recognize and acknowledge that fact.

"What do you feed this guy?" he joked.

Mom gazed at her boy proudly.

"Well, he does pretty much eat us out of house and home," she laughed.

"You know, between his mature good looks and his "substantial" physique, he could easily pass for a 20-year-old and go to any gas station and buy smokes," he chuckled. Wrong words to say to this mom!

"Hey! Don't even suggest it!" said the protective, feisty blonde as she playfully gave Nick a good smack on his forearm.

Everyone there had a good chuckle…at Nick's expense. Trisha remembers that moment as if it had happened yesterday. Nick

William Henderson and Robbie Hummel probably does, too!

One thing is certain. There's a young man who's thankful for a few guys in green and gold who taught him some things about football, and even more thankful for the disciplines of living well that he learned both on and off the field.

Just for the record, Rob, as he now prefers to be called, is now 21, and he doesn't smoke!

By Kathi Rose with memories from Trisha Hummel

CR SO

33 For Doug Evans' Sake

In mid-December 1994, I sat in the Packers locker room at Lambeau Field near the four stalls occupied by the team's starting secondary, Doug Evans, LeRoy Butler, George Teague and Terrell Buckley. The rest of the locker room was virtually empty as most players were in position group meetings. The one scheduled for defensive backs had yet to start. Waiting is a normal part of the job as a NFL reporter. The players I needed to interview after practice were unavailable.

So I made an attempt at small talk, unsure of how well it would be received.

Butler was one of the most talkative players on the team. At times, Buckley was a good interview, but wary of criticism. Teague kept to himself. Evans was always cordial and relaxed compared to the other three higher profile players. The question I asked couldn't have been simpler or more straight forward.

"What are some of your favorite Christmas memories?

There's no way I could have known that the question would have a dramatic effect on my own life.

Butler, Teague and Buckley began recounting memories of years gone by, but Evans wanted no part of it. He withdrew. It was as if he turned to stone. I tucked away what I had just seen. I thought there might be another time to revisit what took place. There was. It came in April at the

Packers' first minicamp following the 1995 draft. Evans remembered the question. He said the reason he didn't answer was that he didn't have any favorite memories.

"It was just another day," he said. "I knew on Christmas I wouldn't be getting any presents."

Evans provided a few more details about his childhood, which prompted me to suggest that I travel to his hometown of Haynesville, LA, following the May minicamp. Evans agreed, but it wasn't until I took the three-flight trip from Green Bay to Detroit to Memphis to Shreveport, La., and showed up at his front door in Bossier City, LA, that he believed it was actually going to take place.

The following day, Evans drove us down a country road near Haynesville to show me a dilapidated and uninhabited 12x60-foot corrugated metal box. Almost all of the windows and screens of the cinder-block supported structure were broken. It had been "home" to Evans and his four brothers and sister for seven years.

"I grew up with poverty all around me, so I just figured what we were going through was normal until I got out of the house and saw that people shouldn't be living like that. It's hard for people to comprehend. They don't understand where I came from. They can't. They don't know how bad it was."

The house, if it could even be called such, cost $25 a month to rent. Amenities were few. Evans remembered walking to a near-by stream with five-gallon buckets to fetch water. One winter, the family lived without heat or electricity. He said when it rained you stood a better chance of staying dry by going outside rather than being inside. Sleeping quarters were cramped. Four brothers shared one bed. Doug slept between the two oldest, Dennis and Norris. When asked about it what it was like, Dennis fought back tears. Doug said he just couldn't talk about it.

"You block things out because you don't want to remember them," he said. "You appreciate things more now because there were times when you didn't know where your next meal was coming from. You would run out of groceries for the month and that was it. There were just so many different things, things that are just part of everyday life that most people take for granted that we couldn't."

As a well-paid professional football player, Evans admitted his favorite and most frequented restaurants in Green Bay and Louisiana were the all-you-can-eat variety. Evans' father, Morrell, was present but worked only sporadically. His older brothers served as his father figures while his mother Emma, whom Evans' sister Nicole called "the greatest person in the world," held the family together the best way she could. Evans, who was a sixth-round draft pick in 1993, used his $38,000 signing bonus to purchase his mother a house.

"It was hard," Emma told me later. "I had a husband who didn't care, but I stayed with him. I just worked and prayed and we stuck together. The older ones would help the younger ones and things got better. I was still praying. I was still holding my faith. That always remained alive in my heart that it was going to get better."

"People ask me, 'How'd you raise your children?' And I would say with faith, love and prayer and that's all that I know. We loved one another. My boys loved me. My daughter loves me. That's what we lived off of. That's all we had."

After driving back to his home in a well-manicured neighborhood in Boosier City, Evans had a chance to reflect on reliving his past.

"The way I look at it, I already lived the worst part of my life," Evans said. "Nothing that happens now can compare. It can never be as bad as it was. That's why I'm so low key. That's why nothing bothers me. It made me tougher. But it's difficult to explain to anyone."

"Now I did. It's the first real chance I had to tell my story," he said after a long, thoughtful pause.

On my return trip to Green Bay, I had ample time to digest what I had seen and heard. When I saw my wife, Jill, I immediately told her to "never let me complain about anything ever again." Possessions, status, money, etc., suddenly held less importance somehow.

Many Christians are familiar with what Paul wrote from prison in his letter to the Philippians. "I know what it is to be in need, and I know what it is to have plenty. I have learned the secret of being content in any and every situation."

In the years since, being content in every situation hasn't always been the easiest thing to do with deaths of family members, losing a job, financial challenges, the recession and dealing with the daily struggles of diabetes. Then I think back to Evans, the painful emptiness of his Christmases, and his suffering because of poverty, the likes of which most Americans can't begin to fathom.

Evans played a key role as a starter on the Packers' Super Bowl XXXI championship and Super Bowl XXXII teams. In 1998, he signed a $22.5 million contract with Carolina. It was the second largest deal for a cornerback at that time (behind Deion Sanders). Injuries hampered his career, including his stops in Seattle and Detroit. I remember when he signed his lucrative free agent deal. It was impossible to look at him as one of those "rich" athletes. Instead, I thanked the Lord for blessing him and his family after all they had been through.

I often think back to sitting in that locker room. It was a routine question on an ordinary day. Yet it provided me with an extraordinary lesson for a lifetime.

By Brad Zimanek

CR ഇ

34 Rawhide, Roger & The Way Outfitters

In 1966 Bart and Cherry Starr agreed to join John and Jan Gillespie in developing a ranch for teenage young men referred by Wisconsin juvenile courts. The details of how this occurred, the miracles that surround it and the story of Jan encouraging John to make contact with Bart are inspiring.

Rawhide Boys Ranch has become one of the most successful facilities of its kind. Youth professionals from around the world come to Rawhide to learn how they achieve an impressive 80% success rate with juveniles. A partnership has developed with a children's program from northern Russia with staff visiting each other's programs every few years. One troubled young man who was a part of Rawhide is Roger Devenport. If his name sounds familiar, it may be because he was featured in *Leap of Faith 3: The Packer Hall of Faith* (Sept. 1998). In one chapter we learned that Roger had become a successful businessman, husband, father and a follower of Christ. But the story has gotten better.

In 1992, Roger and his wife Sue bought 1,100 acres in northern Wisconsin called the Three Lakes Preserve. It needed a great deal of work, but they built up a herd of 500 head of white-tailed deer and nearly 100 trophy buck. In the late '90s, while hunting in Utah, Roger met Cameron Tribolet who had hosted dozens of disabled youth on hunts. Cam is himself disabled, having lost both his legs when shot in an attempted carjacking. Cameron has since partnered with the Devenports to bring numerous disabled youth to the Northern Wisconsin preserve for free hunts.

For many years the Devenports donated lodging, meals and hunts for dozens of youth, inspired in part by knowing the value of these experiences given that Roger had spent so much time away from his family in a youth home. Three Lakes Preserves was sold in 2007, freeing the Devenports to dedicate their time to Way Outfitters in order to help hundreds of disabled and terminally ill youth and American veterans. Long time friends John and Jan Gillespie, Roger's house parents when he was placed at Rawhide, were asked to help set up the federally approved charity and to raise money needed to cover guest costs.

Roger and Sue currently volunteer all of their time providing adventures to youth and veterans from across the country. In fact, everyone at The Way Outfitters is a volunteer. John and Jan continue to serve on the board, raise funds and help in other ways. The Activities Director is Cameron Tribolet.

You can imagine the inspiring stories of persevering through adversity from the guests The Way Outfitters take on hunting, fishing, skiing or other outdoor adventures. Discover Mediaworks, a television production company, became so motivated they provided the time and talent to accompany a fishing trip off the Florida Keys, with guest Corporal Catlin Mixon. Catlin is an Iraq vet who lost his legs in a roadside bomb attack. They produced a heartwarming pilot that is an example of what may soon be a national television series. To view the pilot video and learn about being an advertiser on the show, go to www.TheWayOutfitters.com, click on The Way Outfitters Adventures, National TV Series.

Good ideas always attract good people, and this organization is no exception. Green Bay Packer linebacker A.J. Hawk and his wife Laura are now supporting the cause in various ways, including as spokespersons and going on hunts. So the Packer and Rawhide connection continues to weave a beautiful tapestry to serve as a reminder to all of us about the influence that a few servants, many in green-and-gold, can make.

By Steve Rose with details from John Gillespie

CR SO

35 Ball Boy to the Booth

Kevin showed up for work at 1265 Lombardi Avenue in Green Bay as team ball boy. His father had also secured a job with the team after working in St. Louis. A new coach, Dan Devine, was also making his way into his new office there. Dan's son would be a ball boy, too. There were a lot of new kids on the block that year. Joe Hanner and Zeke Bratkowski's son, Bob, were the veteran ball boys. Kevin got to hang with Bart Starr Jr., who came from pretty good stock, as well.

Nearly 40 years after landing a youngster's dream job, the 50-yr-old Kevin Harlan's recognizable voice booms with excitement as he recounts the tale of his journey into Packer heaven. Harlan's time in Green Bay morphed into realizing more of his dream, culminating in a prominent professional broadcaster's career. His voice is on CBS NFL broadcasts, and now regularly on Westwood One for Monday Night Football with Boomer Esiason. His resume is lengthy.

Harlan also calls NCAA college basketball on CBS, and he can be heard during NBA season chatting with Doug Collins as he calls games for cable channel TNT. He acknowledges that one of the most fun and challenging things is doing the Green Bay Packer Preseason television. You'd think that the national broadcasts would be tougher to do, but not necessarily.

"Because the Green Bay Packer fans are so knowledgeable," Kevin pointed out, "you'd better know your roster, and know it well, or they'll 'call you' on it. It's the greatest honor to do those games with Rich Gannon."

His early years in Green Bay hold nothing but shining memories for

Kevin. He recalled the different players he had the joy of serving, whether it was grabbing some Gatorade for a player, moving blocking dummies, getting towels, or changing cleats on spikes. The jobs he performed and the personalities he was exposed to during those very formative years created numerous memories that he loves to talk about.

"John Brockington was a nice man, and MacArthur Lane was a larger-than-life personality to me."

The job had its occasional downside, and Kevin did witness an occasional family squabble.

"One time Mac and Jim Carter, a nasty linebacker, got into it, screaming at the top of their lungs at one another. It scared the daylights out of me, but for the most part things were pleasant in the locker room," recalls Harlan.

Kevin brought up names like Barty Smith, Jim Del Geizo, who was going to rescue the quarterback position in the mid '70s, and also John Hadl, another quarterback with potential.

"I remember John came in on a private jet. That was really rare in those days, but definitely very cool."

"I also worked with Lynn Dickey and Kenny Payne, who was gonna clean up the receiver position," he recalled.

Kevin is one of the few and the proud to have served in Green Bay from the field and then, later, in the press box.

"I would sneak up to the press box, lock the door, and then pretend to do play-by-play as if I were on the radio. I never would have imagined that my broadcast career would have turned out this way, doing Packer games. It's just the best."

I asked Harlan to share some thoughts on why NFL players often project images of themselves that are sometimes questionable. I hoped he could help bridge the gap of understanding between the mortal fan and the locker room greats.

"The guys can be a bit stand-offish, it's true. I think it's because there are so many demands on their time, and the professional challenges they're facing are enormous and stressful. There's so much at stake in the early part of their career, a lot is on the line. Add to that the fact that many of these guys have never had to work this hard, their bodies are hurting, and they're exhausted," he explained.

I mentioned, at the beginning of this story, that Kevin's father had also begun his career with the Packers in 1971. Of course, only those living on another planet wouldn't know that Kevin's father is Bob who, like his son, is one of the nicest people in the world, married to an equally special woman, Madeline. While we were on the subject of family, this seemed like a good time to talk about keeping priorities in order while living in the sports world.

"When I fly into Green Bay to do a game, I've already done the bulk of the prep work. All the 'hay is in the barn,' so to speak. Dad comes to pick me up from the airport, but we don't go to the field. We go right to Tony Romas for ribs."

Harlan has been married to his love, Ann, since 1987. When he's not on the road, living out of a suitcase, he and Ann call Kansas City home. Of their four children, two are in college, and two are in high school. Kevin has two brothers, Bryan and Michael.

As I was about to begin my interview with Kevin for this chapter, I was interrupted by Kevin, but what I heard made the interruption well worthwhile.

"Steve, hang on a second. 'Honey, drive safely, and be sure to put your seat belt on! I love you!'"

Kevin Harlan is living his dreams, but he definitely has his priorities in order.

By Steve Rose with memories from Kevin Harlan

CR ЯO

36 LeRoy Butler Did It

It was a Thursday night in early fall of 2009. I was watching a local newscast and caught a story about LeRoy Butler, former #36 and All Pro Safety for the Green Bay Packers. Mr. Butler had just purchased the local Ford Dealership located in rural, Waupaca, WI. As the story unfolded, I could feel the excitement building in me. I had heard whisperings about Mr. Butler purchasing the dealership, and now it was being confirmed, but more than that, I knew this story was a "sign."

Earlier in the week I had been in a meeting with a group of local small business owners and business leaders who were brainstorming about potential guest speakers for an upcoming small business and entrepreneur networking event. We expected to draw hundreds of people to the event, yet we had a minimal budget for a keynote speaker. Because the event was planned to take place in Green Bay that December, a tie-in with a former Green Bay Packer who had become a small business owner or entrepreneur after retiring from the NFL would be a good draw. The problem? None of us were connected to any of the retired Packers, or any of the current Packers, for that matter. I left that meeting with the task of identifying and connecting with potential speakers who met our criteria.

By the time our next meeting rolled around, I had assembled a list of former Packers turned business owners. After reviewing and discussing the list, we all agreed to secure LeRoy Butler. The others had also heard of Mr. Butler's purchase of a car dealership. We all felt certain he'd have a great story about his path from the NFL to an entrepreneur. This event was a regional economic development event and Waupaca County is one of the 18 counties in the region, so the Waupaca angle was perfect. I left the meeting with a new task, connect with Mr. Butler and ask if he'd be interested.

A few phone calls led to some referrals to people who knew Mr. Butler. I reached mostly voice mails, so I left kind and professional messages requesting a call back if they thought they could help. One of the people I knew agreed that getting Leroy as the guest speaker would be great. Although she knew people who knew him, she suggested I Google him to see who was representing him in order to make the connection. Getting in contact with Mr. Butler was going to be harder than I had imagined. My mantra became, "If it's meant to be, it will happen. If not, we'll execute plan B."

A week or so passed and then I saw the news story. I felt certain it was a sign that I should stay positive about connecting with Mr. Butler. I went to sleep that night thinking, "If it's meant to be, it will be…."

The next morning, as I passed through Wild Rose on my commute to Appleton, I had this thunderbolt of an idea. Why not turn north, head to Waupaca, and stop at the new Leroy Butler Ford? If Mr. Butler was there, perhaps I could meet him and ask him if he'd be interested in speaking at our event. I'd like to think I had a choice about continuing east, or turning and heading north, but I didn't. Something compelled me to do it. My morning was free of meetings, so I called the office to let my assistant, Jill, know I was making a detour trip to Waupaca before I came in that morning.

The excitement in me was growing, although there was an undercurrent of calm and peacefulness. I knew I had made the right choice. I arrived at the dealership a little before 9 a.m. on a crisp, sunny, Wisconsin fall morning. I felt confident as I opened the door and went in. I was greeted by an upbeat and friendly salesman. I shared my name and requested a few minutes of Mr. Butler's time, if he was available.

Only a few moments later I was greeted by Mr. Butler himself. He ushered me to his office and took a seat behind his desk. Seated opposite him, I took a deep breath, smiled and calmly shared why I was there. LeRoy was kind, attentive and interested in what I had to say. He told me he appreciated how hard it was to start a business. We discussed a few specific challenges he had faced during his own start-up phase. He assured me he would think about helping us out and, once he checked his calendar, he'd get back to me.

I left that meeting feeling certain he was going to help us. When I got to the office and shared with a colleague what I had done, he commented, "You mean, you cold-called LeRoy Butler?"

"Yes, I guess that's exactly what I did" I said, smiling from ear to ear.

A few months later, I had the final task and great delight of introducing Mr. Butler to hundreds of small business owners and entrepreneurs at our event.

By Amy Pietsch

CR SO

37 Humbled, Healthy & Happy

Tony Mandarich knows there's probably nothing he can do or say to the fans to remove the bitter taste of the memories he left behind after his unproductive years in Green Bay. Labeled by Sports Illustrated as "The Incredible Bust" three years after they had shown his steroid-laced form on the cover of their magazine was enough shame for him to bear.

At present, the man born in 1966 in Oakville, Ontario, is experiencing his greatest winning streak ever, and it isn't on the field. It began outside of Detroit on March 23, 1995, when his life hit bottom, thankfully while he was still living. I believe Tony's been "beat up" enough. My reason for sharing his story is to offer some redemption.

Tony was taken with the second pick in the '89 NFL draft by the Packers, right after Troy Aikman. Left on the table was Barry Sanders. It's understandable some would become agitated at the premise that the Packers would still be winning Super Bowls if we had chosen Sanders, but...

Tony is the first to admit that he was a prideful and arrogant know-it-all on steroids when he made the crack in negotiations that Green Bay was a "village." Still, he held out, hoping to get "Aikman type money." He regrets that, as he does so many other things he said and did during that time.

I was told by someone in the Packer organization that the Packers knew Mandarich was "on the juice" (taking steroids) when they took him. That was quite obvious even to most novices who had no clue what steroids actually were. Things would change when Tony got to the NFL, and he knew it.

"The testing in the NFL was different, more thorough, and I knew I couldn't get away with the things that I did when I was in college. I stopped taking steroids, but I increased my pain killers and alcohol. Then I had the thyroid problem, and I ended up living quite a big lie and had to put on quite a façade," he confessed.

Mandarich was sent packing after his contract expired in '92. He has nothing, however, but great things to say about the fans and the organization.

"The Green Bay fans were great to me. They're such down-to-earth people. I could relate to them. James Campen was a great teammate and Kenny Ruettgers was a real 'stand up' guy."

Once he hit his 'bottom,' things actually started looking up. He decided to sober up from everything, painkillers and alcohol. He's been stone sober ever since.

"I don't do drugs or drink socially. It's been the best time of my life. It's an easier way to live. With sobriety came the ability to "feel" again. What came next was the regret of how I handled myself in Green Bay. I feel badly that I was not grateful for the time there," he admitted.

Eleven months into his sobriety, an opportunity came to play for the Indianapolis Colts. He would have never thought it was possible, but he rationalized that if he could get sober, he could do anything. Today he, and his second wife, Char, are living their dreams in Arizona as co-owners of a photography and internet marketing company. He speaks to schools and companies about the addiction process, and offers his help to counselors and law enforcement personnel who work with addicts.

It's great news that one who had fallen so far down could be lifted up and redeemed. As one who has been clean and sober for nearly 20 years now, I get it. I wanted to say as much to Tony.

"Tony, you've been 'beat up' enough. That's not what this story is going to be about. We all goof up, some of us in a big and public way. My hope is to use your story of pride, humility and redemption so that the Packer faithful can hear it. As an ex- drunk, saved by grace, I want you to know I'm proud of you."

"Thanks, Steve," he said in that low voice that any world-class broadcaster should envy.

Other writers have covered the "old" Tony Mandarich, with all of the accompanying garbage. There's a new Tony, one who has peace of mind and a healthy life. That's one story we think is worth telling.

By Steve Rose with memories from Tony Mandarich

38 A Purple 4Shadowing

It was 1980, and I was 15. My friend Dawn and I were glued to the TV in our Hilbert, WI, living room for the Packers/Bears game. There was very little left of my fingernails when the game was tied 6-6 in overtime. You true Packer history buffs know how the game ended. I'll never forget chuckling and hooting and hollering about

Chester Marcol's famous touchdown. While that was memorable, what followed the game for me was unforgettable.

We heard the neighbor boys from across the street celebrating the victory outside and hurried out to join them. We had a pool table in our basement, so we invited the guys in to play a couple post-Packer-victory pool games. When we finished, I started throwing the remaining pool balls into the pockets, not realizing one of my neighbors was doing the same at the opposite end of the table. At very high speed, one of the balls he was throwing and one that I was throwing collided.

The purple ball flew through the air and smashed right into my teeth . . . not a good way for a girl to start her sophomore year of high school.

When my mind drifts back to that day, I don't dwell on the resulting root canal or dental crowns. I think of the Packers and of the fun we have because of them. And I think about the purple four ball. Who knew something purple with a 4 on it could be that dangerous? Hmm, a 4shadowing of things to come nearly 30 years later?

By Betsy Rozelle

CR ৪০

39 Greeted By Bark Starr

While I love screaming in the stands at Lambeau with the best of them, you might call me a fair-weather fan. Oh, I'll stick by the Pack even when they're on a long losing streak, but my favorite games are those played in good weather. A pre-season game on a 75-degree sunny August afternoon suits me far more than a championship game in 20-degree weather in December.

That said, I've got a few stories about the Packers that I'm sure a die-hard fan would kill for.

In the 1970s, the Starrs lived on land my dad's parents once farmed, around the corner from LeBrun Street in De Pere, WI, just a few blocks from my grandmother's house on Webster Avenue. In the heyday of the Packers' Super Bowl years, when I was about 10, my sister D'Ann, a cousin and I walked from my grandmother's home down a couple blocks to Bart Starr's house for autographs. Their black lab came bounding at us from the yard and bit my sister on the hand.

We knocked on the door and Bart's wife, Cherry, answered. She invited us in, washed D'Ann's hand and put a Band-Aid on it. Bart then took us into his office and signed some photographs for us. The bookcases were filled with trophies, the walls lined with awards, and the Starrs showered us with old-fashioned Southern hospitality. The best part was the Starrs didn't seem to mind at all when my sister and I went back the very next day with more cousins for more autographs. That year I got a No. 15 Jersey for my birthday and wore it all summer.

The Packers have always been a part of everyday life for people in Green Bay. My dad, Raphael LeBrun, remembers peddling newspapers in De Pere for some of the Packers in the '50s, including "the Gray Ghost," Tony Canadeo, and fullback Clarke Hinkle. Tobin Rote, quarterback before Starr, lived two doors down. Dad has fond memories of going to games at the original stadium on the east side of Green Bay.

Bart Starr has always been close to the fans, doing charity work, leading parades, and promoting worthy causes, especially at Rawhide, a home for wayward young men. My maternal grandfather, Alton Hutchison, once owned the land now owned by Rawhide. He logged it during the Depression years until all the lumber was depleted, and then he sold it.

Tom Hutchison, integral in founding the Packers Hall of Fame during his years as manager of Channel 11 (when it was a new ABC affiliate) in Green Bay, has a treasure trove of stories about the Packers. My favorite is the one he tells about the time when, just out of college as a cub reporter for a small Waupaca newspaper, he was recruited to drive Bart Starr's new red Corvette from Green Bay to Rawhide for a charity event.

At the time, it was understood that a new car should never exceed 50 mph for the first 500 miles. Tom drove slowly down the country roads to New London, but by the time he got to Mosquito Hill, he was itching to see what that car could really do. He put the pedal down and flew at 125 mph the last nine miles (or so he says). Though he had encountered Starr many times since then, it wasn't until recently (2009) that Tom finally shared the story with him. The two had a good laugh together.

For many families in Northeast Wisconsin, every Sunday afternoon revolved around the games. Cousins, aunts and uncles and grandparents all crowded into the living room immediately after the big noon meal and gathered around the TV. Often, we would spot people we knew when the camera panned the stands.

Screaming and carrying on was par for the course, shouting "Touchdown!" and "Interception!" with the same intensity week after week. So, when I was 7 and 8 years old, watching the Packers play in the Super Bowl on TV, I didn't realize just how big it was. Could my family shout any louder than they had during the pre-season games back in August?

During half-time, we kids would run all around the yard tossing a football. I didn't understand why my dad would get so angry when we took a particular football to play with from its special place in the living room. After all, it was just a football covered with handwriting.

When I was finally old enough to know better, however, I took a closer look at it. It was autographed by all the Packers and coaches who won the 1965 National Football League Championship: Bart Starr, Vince Lombardi, Ray Nitschke, Jerry Kramer, Max McGee, Paul Horning, Willie Wood. It's a wonder we hadn't destroyed it. My mother won the football in a contest by filling in the blank, "I love going to Packer games because ..." She answered, "It's quieter than staying home with five kids." (She had two more after that.)

Of course, the requisite to get into a championship game was to have season tickets. To get those you have be on the waiting list for decades, or know someone with tickets who can't attend. Until a few years ago, season tickets stayed with a family, similar to an inheritance. Now, they often go up for purchase when somebody dies.

A few of our extended family members owned season tickets, but it was tough to score them for championship games. I called my dad to ask him how he managed to get tickets to the 1996 championship Green Bay game that December.

"Well, you know," he said, lowering his voice to a sympathetic tone, "Uncle Frank died."

Packer memories accumulate over the years. Recently, I've had the pleasure to attend the Welcome Back Packers luncheon in the Lambeau Atrium. Community members buy seats at tables and then names of Packer players are randomly drawn from a hat corresponding with table numbers.

My favorite lunch mate was Charles Woodson in 2006. I'm embarrassed to say that nobody at my table, least of all me, knew his name at the time. I am proud, however, to say that Charles and I discussed the fact that we were both taking piano lessons.

As Woodson's talent became strikingly evident that year (as a cornerback, not a pianist), I took to shouting "There's my lunch buddy!" whenever his name was called in a game. I must say, it's a great way to annoy, if not outright embarrass, your teen-agers. I think of it as my contribution in helping them acquire their own memories for another Packer book someday!

By Margaret LeBrun
Co-Publisher/Executive Editor, Insight Publications

ଔ ଌ

40 On a Mission to See the Packers

Our eyeglass mission trip to Honduras was set well before we knew the Green Bay Packers would be facing the New York Giants in the playoffs in January 2008. We decided to pack our treasured jerseys and other "Cheesehead attire" to be worn that Sunday in our makeshift eye care clinic, located hours deep in the rainforest. All day long the people of the village would ask about our clothing, not understanding why we were all dressed in green and gold. It felt as if someone had rubbed salt in the wound, certain as we were that there would be no chance to learn the outcome of the game until returning home the next week.

Our fearless mission trip leader, Dr. Mark Ebben of Kaukauna, had faith that his short-wave radio would bring in the much-anticipated game. At the close of a long day in which we provided eye exams and glasses to the needy people of the region, he climbed the closest mountain in an attempt to get a signal. Nothing. We were heartsick. We all made futile attempts to enjoy our evening meal, knowing kickoff was only minutes away, and we were thousands of miles away.

Suddenly, Father Angelo, a resident of the village and our host for the 10-day trip, burst into the room.

"I believe I have your football game on the television!" he blurted out with his Maltese/Spanish/English accent.

We screamed with delight. Then it dawned on us. What television?

We had barely sufficient amounts of electricity to run the equipment in our clinic and, at certain times of the day, only sporadically. How could Father possibly have the game, our game, on a television we didn't even know existed in the middle of the Honduran rain forest?

We literally ran to his adobe home to discover, incredulously, that he did indeed have the game in Spanish on his TV. There was some interference (snow) on the screen, but it was difficult to distinguish between that and the real snow that was coming down in Green Bay. Frankly, we didn't care. We were watching the game!

The cheering and screaming coming from Father's home drew a large crowd of villagers who had gathered on the dirt road outside. They had to be seriously wondering what was happening inside. Our frivolity continued to the bitter end as Brett Favre threw that last, fateful pass and, just as our family and friends thousands of miles to the north were doing,

Mary Harp-Jirschele (Favre jersey) in Honduras

we, too, mourned the end of the season.

But we were grateful, so very grateful, that on an eye glass mission trip thousands of miles away, we were miraculously able to see our beloved Packers.

By Mary Harp-Jirschele

ভে ৫০

41 The 16 Million $ Man

The year was 1995. Ken Ruettgers and I were pre-recording a segment of our weekly Timeout radio show that ran during the football season in Green Bay. We'd just finished up a live show and now we were going to put one "in-the-can" for the following week's program because the team would be playing a Monday night game that week.

"Whose gonna be on with us, Ken?" I asked as we went down the hall to the soda machine.

Before Ken could answer I looked up to see a huge, burly young man sporting a flattop haircut. He was grinning widely. Ken made the introduction.

"Steve, this is Adam Timmerman."

"Hi, how are things in Iowa?" I asked.

Having done my homework on all the fellows on the team, I knew that Adam was from Cherokee, a town in western Iowa with a population of 7,000.

"Good, thanks for asking."

I like to think my casual but sincere conversation helped to settle his nerves a bit. Not only was he a rookie on the field, but he was also a novice who was completely out of his comfort zone when it came to being on live radio. We settled into the studios and the offensive lineman went on to tell our audience that he felt well-grounded because of his wife, Jana. He spoke of his humble beginnings on the farm in Iowa, and the importance of his Christian faith.

Once we had finished, I offered Adam what I thought was some rather sound advice. I pulled him aside into one of the offices just outside the studio. I should mention here that the advice I was about to administer came on the heels of my own bankruptcy. That experience definitely colored the way I looked at business ventures. Besides that, I honestly thought it would be no time and this kid would be back on the combine in Cherokee. I didn't tell him that, but I admit that's what I was thinking.

"Adam, I'd like to respectfully recommend that you be wise with the money you're making here. It's a great opportunity."

He listened carefully and politely as I went on to encourage him not to be one of the guys who "blows it all" on expensive tastes. He hesitated before speaking.

"I think, if you knew my wife, you'd know that we're very frugal people, so you don't have to worry about that with us, though I appreciate where you're coming from," he said kindly and quite graciously.

Maybe the conversation hadn't been necessary, but I felt better having had it.

We said our goodbyes. Little would any of us have known then that this man of character would become a starter on the team who, along with Jana, would do memorable Chevy commercials on TV.

Adam and I shared some great moments together, as he was a regular guest on both my radio and TV show over the next two years. If I saw him today, I'd probably tease him about being a South Dakota State Jack Rabbit.

But the one moment in time I most remember came in 2000. I was listening to a Green Bay sports radio channel.

"And Adam Timmerman has signed a contract with the St. Louis Rams that will pay him $16 million dollars over four years."

Wow! I shook my head and laughed out loud, remembering that conversation in 1995. I wonder if Adam was glad that a farm boy from Eden, WI, had encouraged another farm boy only five years earlier to save his pennies?

And I remember thinking, "He sure won't be pinching pennies anymore….nickels and dimes, maybe, but definitely not pennies!"

By Steve Rose

CR SO

42 Who Was That Kid in Here?

Chuck Freimund has a confession to make to the Green Bay Packers. It's that in 1981, when he was in the locker room covering his heroes, he was only 14 years old. He graduated from Martin Luther High School in 1985. Chuck, a self-proclaimed die-hard Packer nut, still enjoys being a part of the media who have access to the team.

The 43-year-old told me, during my visit with him, that he recalls growing up in Greendale, a suburb of Milwaukee, in an era when Packers weren't as big a deal as they currently are. He also pointed out a fact that most people have forgotten.

"In the '70s, the Packers weren't must-see TV like they are today. It was pretty common for Milwaukee County Stadium, because seating wasn't sold out, to prevent the game from being broadcast in the Milwaukee area where I lived. Every so often, enough game tickets would be sold, and the blackout would be lifted," he recalls.

He has his opinion as to when the wheel of fortune turned in Titletown.

"I believe the future of the team changed for the better in 1989 under the helm of quarterback Don Majkowski. What an exciting season that was! The team went 10-6 with a couple of key instant-replay games. They nearly made the playoffs. Don still gets lots of mileage from the replay against the Bears for his touchdown pass to Sterling Sharpe."

Chuck would later host a radio talk show with "Magic Man" Don Majkowski, whose notoriety among Green Bay fans may be more for getting hurt and losing his job to someone named Favre in 1992.

Since his childhood, Chuck has aspired to be a member of the media who would cover the green-and-gold warriors. His first year in the biz was 1983, when the 16-year-old got a job with WAUK Milwaukee. They covered both Lambeau Field and Milwaukee County Stadium (where the Packers played four games each season until 1994). He made an astounding $15 per game.

Chuck rode to the games with Bruce Marcus, Larry Bandy and John Reynolds. I'm not sure, but I thought there was a policy that media personnel had to be at least 18 to get into the press box and locker rooms, but maybe not.

"I was a tall kid, 6'1" or 6'2" so I could easily pass for about 22," Chuck remembers. "I'd always get to ask one or two questions. There was one day, though, when he saw something very wild happen in the locker room.

"After an '83 game, in which the Packers pounded Tampa Bay, Bud Lea from the Milwaukee Sentinel asked Tampa coach John McKay why his team 'stunk.'"

There was a momentary, reflective pause before Chuck continued his conversation with me.

"And McKay says, 'Get away from me or I'll punch you in the mouth!'"

"That was quite a moment. I'd played for a coach who did lots of yelling so I really wasn't staggered by it at all. But nothing like that has even happened in the last twenty-seven years, thank goodness," laughed the radio vet. (By the way, McKay would later apologize to Lea when the teams met in Tampa later that season.)

"Was there ever a favorite game for you?" I quizzed.

"You bet. October 1983, the Packers played the Redskins on Monday Night Football. My parents drove me up to Green Bay. We stopped at the Packer Inn just long enough to register. Then we headed directly to the stadium," he replied without a moment's hesitation.

There was one incident, as he recalls, that was somewhat bizarre.

"I remember seeing a bunch of really big fellows hanging around just outside the press box, so I asked someone in the press box, 'Hey, who are those guys?'"

"Without missing a beat, or so much as a flinch of any facial muscle, the answer flies back at me, 'Those are Howard Cosell's body guards.' I admit. I was impressed."

"As for the game itself, the offenses were outstanding while the defenses for either team couldn't stop a soul if their lives depended on it. Mark Moseley of the Skins missed a chip shot field goal at the gun, allowing the Packers to slip away with a 48-47 victory. To this day, that's the highest number of points ever scored in MNF lore. It was sheer mania on the field. I didn't get a call in to my parents to come get me to bring me back to the motel until nearly 3 a.m."

Chuck graduated high school in '86 and the age issue, which

apparently had never been a factor, never would. He still loves his craft to this day, and is proud of the fact that he's one of the longest tenured sports broadcasters in the state of Wisconsin.

Chuck currently works for Sports Radio 1250 WSSP in Milwaukee, and acknowledges it's the best job he's ever had. He makes no bones about the fact that he loves what he does and he is very grateful.

"Steve, how many people get to live their dream as I have? I get to cover the Green Bay Packers!"

Chuck's right. Not too many folks have had the joy of going to a job they love, much less to a job that gives one access to the Green Bay Packers. Now, of course, he makes slightly more than $15 a game! Doesn't get any better than that, does it?

By Steve Rose with memories from Chuck Freimund

CR SO

43 A Packer-Cowboy Love Affair

Football. It brings people together, at least it's supposed to. There's nothing quite like getting together with a group of friends on a Sunday afternoon to watch a football game. It's even better if you happen to be lucky enough to score tickets to the game. You laugh. You eat some of your favorite tailgate foods. You cheer your team on to victory. You celebrate when your team wins. You console each other when they lose.

I have always been a Packer fan. It didn't matter that while growing up I lived closer to the Chicago Bears than the Green Bay Packers. I was a Wisconsinite, and my heart pumped green and gold.

When I met Karmen, the woman who was to become my wife, I discovered, to my shock, that not only was she was not a Packer fan, but she was, in fact, a diehard Dallas Cowboys fan! She lived and breathed football every bit as much as I did, but her blood ran blue and silver, colors that are anything but popular in Packerland.

Wanting to impress Karmen during our courtship, I bought a Cowboys sweatshirt. Needless to say, she was thrilled! I even wore it sometimes! (I had convinced myself that my respect for Coach Tom Landry made it ok to buy it. Truth is, of course, I really just wanted to impress my lady.)

Karmen and I were married in October 1995. Little did we realize how quickly the Cowboy-Packer rivalry would rear its ugly head. The day after our wedding the Packers travelled to play Dallas in Texas Stadium, only to lose 34-24. Fortunately, the distraction of our honeymoon allowed us to take it all in stride.

The rest of the season, however, was a little rough, to say the least. Dallas and Green Bay were both having great seasons and the tension in our home was palpable on game days. I wanted her to join me in watching the Packers, but she would have none of it. She actually expected me to (gasp) watch the Cowboys!

To add insult to injury, Karmen was shocked to learn that my Dallas Cowboy sweatshirt was a mere ploy to "get the girl," and as both of us had extremely high hopes that our respective team would come out on top, we found we spent every Sunday bickering over football.

Later that year, the rivalry really came to a head. It was January 14, 1996, the Conference Championship Game. Green Bay was once again playing Dallas, this time for a trip to the Super Bowl. It was a hard fought game, but Green Bay lost 38-27. We were watching the game with Karmen's brother, who was beyond frustrated with the game. He decided to turn the game off, totally oblivious to the fact that Karmen was cheering for the Cowboys. What was supposed to be a fun game of football had turned into a major family feud.

The Cowboys went on to win the Super Bowl. Naturally, Karmen was elated, but she now admits that much of the fun had been taken out of the game by the stress it caused in our home on game days.

Our first football season together had been rough. And while Karmen loved her Cowboys, she decided she cared more about keeping peace in our home, so she decided to convert. Yes, she became a Packer fan, which proves "God is a Packer fan," since only He could have healed the rift between this otherwise happy couple, and convert a lifelong Cowboy fan!

Obviously, it didn't hurt that the next season the Green Bay Packers won the Super Bowl. Karmen had converted at the perfect time, and ended up being as avid a fan of the Packers as she had been for the Cowboys. Together we now watch Packer games every season. We've even attended a couple of home games. There's nothing quite like being at Lambeau on game day! Everybody around you becomes an immediate best friend!

Earlier I mentioned that football can bring people together. For me, it did in more ways than one. I used to work in radio in Wisconsin's Fox Valley with this book's author, Steve Rose. By now a die-hard Packer fan, Karmen happened across the book *Leap of Faith: God Must Be a Packer Fan* in a Christian bookstore and purchased it. The book was written by none other than my radio buddy, Steve Rose. Not only did I enjoy reading the book, but it became the impetus to look up my old friend.

Later that year Steve came to Mauston on his *God Must Be a Packer Fan* book tour. It was so great to catch up with him that we invited him to stay with us the next time he was in the area. Steve took us up on that offer when he returned to speak in the nearby city of Tomah. We had the best time together. In fact, we stayed up almost the entire night talking and listening to music.

With barely two hours of sleep, Steve awoke to prepare for his speaking engagement at Lighthouse Assembly of God Church in Tomah when he realized he had left his dress pants at home! What he learned later that day was that they had fallen off the hanger in his living room in Neenah. While he didn't look as "put together" as he normally did on speaking engagements, he sucked it up and went in wearing a nice white shirt, tie and jeans. It certainly wasn't his usual attire, but the message still got preached and he and the congregation had a great time.

Oh, as for my attire, specifically the Cowboys sweatshirt? I still have it, but it's buried deep inside a cubby hole somewhere in the house. I probably should get rid of it, but it's a part of the history of a time when I brought my wife into the light, the glorious light of Packer green and gold!

By Greg Bernacchi

ભ ৹৭

44 Jet Fans Saw the Light

No matter where you live, you will usually have no difficulty finding another Packer fan. I grew up in Milwaukee where there is no shortage of places to watch the Pack. However, it's only when you leave Wisconsin that you realize how much of a luxury that is. I've lived in the Dallas/Ft. Worth area, Nashville, TN, Cedar Rapids, IA, and most recently San Angelo, TX. No matter what city's it's in, if you walk into a Packer bar, or even an "enemy" establishment, and see even one green and gold jersey, you've got an instant friend. No matter where I travel, or live, the common thread has been to see a stranger wearing a Packer hat or shirt, and to know you've just met up with an extended family member.

Being a Packer fan can mean experiencing a plethora of emotions–joy, sadness, anger, frustration, and hope to name a few. In 1995, however, I learned about good-natured compassion. While living in Nashville, I went to a place called The Box Seat with 20-25 other Packer faithful. Because we had the largest contingency, we were given the main TV. Watching one of the smaller TVs each week was a group of five or six Jets fans.

Working on a 3-13 season, there was little for these guys to cheer about. These fans would wear shirts that vertically had J-E-T-S, and horizontally the rest of the acronym (J)ust (E)nd (T)he (S)eason. Our Packers, meanwhile, were heading to an 11-5 finish. We actually started feeling sorry for them, so we decided to start cheering on the Jets with those guys. In turn, they started cheering on the Pack. It became obvious, over time, that those Jets fans sincerely appreciated the gesture.

I moved from Nashville before the start of the 1996 season, so I don't know whatever happened with those Jets fans. I can only hope they saw the light and became Packer fans for good!

By Ken Franz

CR ßO

45 The Lost Coach

Gary LaFave was the President and Executive Director of Freedom House in Green Bay, a homeless shelter that can accommodate up to 15 families at a time. Freedom House offers programs that help families succeed in the spiritual, physical, emotional and financial areas of life. It's not glamorous work, but much needed and, sadly, the demand continues to grow.

As can be the case for a non-profit organization, funds were getting low at Freedom House. What Freedom House needed was a spokesperson to help them in fundraising efforts, but who could they get? Gary certainly had his "wish list," but he knew that there would have to be divine intervention to pull off making that happen.

In January 2005, Gary began to seriously pray that God would send someone to help them with the financial aspects of Freedom House. Now, six months later, he found himself standing at a July press conference listening to a distinguished man make a plea for others to join him in an effort to keep the efforts of Freedom House alive. Gary was marveling at what God had done as the man spoke to the gathering from the media.

"I tell you that God led me here," he began. "I pray that you will join me in the effort here at Freedom House. This is a wonderful ministry and I am proud to lend my name to it."

How did this gentleman, who was no stranger to anyone in Green Bay, find himself standing at the podium endorsing this great cause? Well, it seems that for the last six months, in one way or another, he kept hearing about the Freedom House. His son was one of those sources.

"Hey, dad, in school today they were talking about Freedom House and the homeless families in our community."

Later that week, he read an article in the paper about Freedom House. Not long after that, he heard commentary on the radio about Freedom House. It was as if there was a "power" making sure he got the message.

He couldn't help but wonder if, perhaps, he was destined to help in some way. He had, of course, convinced himself that he had a great excuse for not being involved. After all, he was incredibly busy and he gets thousands of requests to help other organizations and causes, so what was so special about this one? Then something happened to him that caused him to reassess his thinking and future strategy.

It happened in July. He was on his way back to Green Bay from beautiful Door County, WI. He had spent some much-needed time relaxing, aware that his busiest time of year at work was on the horizon.

Amazingly, (some would say it was bizarre) he got lost in the Northeast part of Green Bay. Hardly a stranger to the community (he had lived there since 2000) he nevertheless found himself to be quite lost. He pulled into a parking lot in order to turn his car around, looked up and saw a sign that read, Freedom House. Next to the sign was a large building with a big white cross on the side of it.

"Okay, God, I get it!" he chuckled to himself as he headed his car in what he believed to be the right direction.

Arriving home safely, the "lost man" picked up the phone and contacted Freedom House. The staff couldn't believe with whom they were speaking! The man requested a tour of their facility.

"When would you like to come over?" asked the staff person.

"Would it be possible to come today?" questioned the caller.

"Absolutely. Come on over. We'll be expecting you."

The tour went well, very well, in fact. He spent about two hours at Freedom House chatting with families and getting to know more about the mission there. Before he left he had a simple but direct question.

"Do you need anything right now?"

"Yes, actually we do. We sure could use a large-screen TV," they asked in faith.

"You'll have one within a week," the man declared without hesitation.

True to his word, the TV arrived within a week.

Just six months after praying for someone to step forward and be a voice for Freedom House, LaFave was attending this unbelievable press conference listening to this man address Green Bay and surrounding area media.

"I'm going to make Freedom House an extension of my family," he told the media.

The man, no doubt, had any number of legitimate excuses to keep him from making any commitment to Freedom House or to any of the thousands of other groups who request his help. He chose, nonetheless, to freely throw his hat in as an "official" spokesperson for Freedom House never questioning the divine orchestration that brought him to this particular moment in his life.

Who was this man "who once was lost," but now could be found at Freedom House lending his name and resources? Well, the locals know him as the coach of a local team, a pretty popular team at that. There, standing at the podium, was none other than Mike Sherman, who was the current head coach of the Green Bay Packers!

By Steve Rose with details from Gary LaFave

CR ЯD

46 That Jean's a Mover

I deal with most of my customers by phone, and then dispatch crews to do the in-home work. The result is that I actually seldom meet my customers, though we often develop great relationships. Packer Kabeer Gbaja Biamila was one such customer with whom I had an enjoyable time over the phone, but never actually met.

A few years back, when Kabeer was still playing with the Packers, I attended the grand opening of a local Citizens Bank. A bank officer that I have known for years was giving me a tour along with my dad, and several of our friends. As we came around a corner, I immediately recognized a familiar face seated at a table signing autographs for the bank's customers. I snuck out of the tour group and got in the KGB line.

It wasn't long before I was at the front of the line.

"Hey, Kabeer! I'm not looking for an autograph. I just wanted to introduce myself. I'm Jean, your mover," I said.

He pulled out his cell phone, punched a button, and turned it toward me to show me his screen, which had "Jean" and my phone number across it.

"This Jean?" he asked, with a big grin.

"Yup," I laughed.

Much to my surprise, he jumped up, came around the table and gave me a huge hug.

"It's so nice to finally meet you after all this time!"

Then he surprised and flattered me.

"Can I get your picture?" he asked.

He gave his phone to one of the gentlemen in line, asking him take a picture of us. Meanwhile, I am desperately looking around for anyone I know to witness this remarkable conversation! Imagine that. KGB wanted my picture!

The fellows who were in line behind me were beginning to grumble. They were still waiting for autographs, so I said good-bye and walked away from the table. Just then, my dad and my other friends came around the corner. I couldn't contain my excitement.

"You're not going to believe this. I just saw Kabeer, and we actually had a quick conversation, and then we had our picture taken together!" I blurted out without taking a breath.

I could tell by the looks on their faces they weren't buying it!

"No, really, I did!" I said as convincingly as I could.

If you ever meet KGB, do me a favor, will you? Ask him if he still has my picture in his phone. Maybe someone will finally believe me!

By Jean Long Manteufel

CR ЮO

47 Jurko the Accordion Man

During the '93-94 NFL season, WMBE, a small radio station in Chilton, WI. broadcasted one of the first Monday Night post-Packer game talk shows of its kind, Pack Rap. Hosted by radio personality John Maino, along with Packer fan favorite defensive lineman, John Jurkovic, the show took place at the Altona Supper Club in New Holstein, WI.

Pack Rap could be heard on 43 radio stations around Wisconsin and Upper Michigan. The format provided an opportunity for listeners and the studio audience, as well, to ask their questions. For some odd reason, I remember that the show's favorite caller was "Larry from Manitowoc."

Isn't it strange the things we remember where our beloved Packers are concerned?

My father, Jerry Schneider, was and is still the leader of his own popular, local German Polka band. He's also still the host of a Saturday morning polka show on WMBE. Throughout the season, it became a running gag that John Jurkovic was taking accordion lessons and his favorite childhood Polka Band was Jerry Petroiczak and the Polka Sharps from Jurko's hometown of Calumet, IL.

As the season wound down and Christmas approached, a friend of my dad came to him with an idea.

"Jerry, why don't you and a few of your guys from the band come in and perform some Christmas music coming in and out of the commercial breaks?"

"You know, that's not a bad idea," agreed Jerry.

It was then that I came up with a funny gag I was confident Jurko would go along with. I shared it with Uncle Chuck and Dad.

"Hey, since Jurko is supposedly taking accordion lessons, let's give him the chance to show off what he's learned so far!" I grinned.

Uncle Chuck's face was covered in a mischievous grin as I spoke. He intuitively knew where I was going with this, and Dad agreed to play along with whatever we had up our sleeves for Jurko. You see, we Schneiders have a few legit accordion players! We would need two accordions if we were going to pull off this spoof. So Dad and Uncle Chuck found and dusted off their instruments.

The plan was that, before the show, Uncle Chuck would take his button box accordion around the corner, out of sight of the audience, and play "Christmas Chop Sticks" into a cordless microphone. At the appropriate time during the show, my brother Jeff strapped an accordion on the unsuspecting Jurko. Then Chuck began to play, but what the audience saw was the big defensive lineman playing! Being a really good sport, Jurko played along with the gag perfectly. The audience was astonished. They loved it and so did he.

I think this story demonstrates the incredible comfort the fans provide for the players, that a defensive lineman could play accordion with the Jerry Schneider German Polka band! This could only have happened with a Packer, and only in Wisconsin!

By Tom Schneider

48 Diamonds in the Restaurant

One of the intriguing aspects of having a few friends who wear or, in this case, wore the green-and-gold was to watch the attention they received. The truth is that the type of attention most of them get is a bit outlandish and, in my opinion, an indication of just how badly our priorities are out of order, but that's for another time, another story.

On January 15 and 16, 2000, I was traveling with Robert Brooks to various engagements and signings. Generally speaking, around the Green Bay area, most of the fellows had few distractions or people bothering them. On the road, however, it was a different story. On one occasion Brooks and I were in the Racine-Kenosha area in southeastern Wisconsin to do a series of church services. We arrived on Saturday night, checked into our hotel, and then headed off to find a nice place to get a bite to eat.

Robert was always eating healthy. Me? Well, I love to eat anything that tastes good which, often times, rules out anything healthy! We chose the Summit Restaurant for our dining pleasure that evening. Once inside, the hostess seated us immediately at a table in the back of the dining room.

"Can I get you each something to drink?" she inquired.

"I'll have a diet cola," I said.

"I'll just have water," replied Robert.

Within minutes our server approached the table. Robert was always dressed very fashionably, and tonight was no exception. Accenting his wardrobe were a sizeable pair of diamonds in his ears, which clearly captured the attention of our server. My suspicion was that he didn't actually recognize Robert himself. His question confirmed my suspicions.

"Wow, those are neat earrings you have, sir. May I ask what you do for a living?"

Robert had a creative, if not somewhat provocative, answer.

"I'm currently unemployed."

Robert had recently retired from the Packers, though by this time he'd confided in me that he was thinking seriously about coming back, and he was hoping to do it with the Packers, though he knew that that would have its challenges.

"I have a friend who's a jeweler and I bet he could get you a few bucks for those if you need the cash."

"Naw, I think for right now I can make it."

"Well, I can get you his information before you leave if you need it. So, what can I get you guys?"

It was then that Robert did an end around that confused me. He told the server we needed a bit more time. Now, I knew what I wanted, and I knew Robert knew what he was going to order, as well.

"Let's go!" Robert said in a somewhat demanding tone.

"What?" I quizzed, seriously confused by his request.

"Let's get out of here," he said even more firmly.

I trusted he knew what he was doing, so I followed him out. When we got to the car he explained himself.

"Steve, here's how it works. Sometimes a server, or even the hostess, will go into the kitchen and tell them that a Packer is in the house. Slowly, but surely, people start to peek out from the kitchen. Then other people at the tables start lookin' and talking. I know that I know we were about to draw a crowd."

I trusted his judgment, but I don't care to have anyone deny me dinner! As it turned out, we ran through the drive-up at McDonalds. Don't get me

wrong. I love Mickey D's, but I had been so looking forward to a quiet and relaxing dinner with my "brother."

Back to the motel we went where we "shot the breeze" while watching ESPN's Sports Center. I ate microwave popcorn as Robert ironed his shirt for the next day's church service.

May I make a suggestion to you? The next time you see a Packer in a restaurant, please give him some time and space,

Steve Rose and Robert Brooks

Diamonds in the Restaurant

for his sake, and even more so for the guy or gal with him who may be in great need of a meal!

By Steve Rose

℞ ℠

49 No Bed Time for Cary

I'm a big Packer fan. Is there anyone from Wisconsin who isn't? I've had the thrill of going to a few games, including the New Orleans Super Bowl. It might surprise you, then, to know that it wasn't my favorite game. Instead, it was the 1983 Packers and Redskins game at Lambeau Field.

I wasn't even at that particular historic and record-breaking Monday Night Football classic, but my parents, Helen and Pat, were. My folks, who were Packer season-ticket holders for Green Bay's old City Stadium before Lambeau Field was even a blueprint, had tickets for that night's game. My younger brother, Charlie, and I were given very specific instructions from our parents before they left for Green Bay.

"Now, boys, you can watch the game until halftime. Then you need to go to bed, okay?" Mom kindly but firmly requested of us.

You can imagine that we weren't too pleased about her restrictions, but we did manage to obligingly grunt something to her to acknowledge that we had heard her. In a matter of moments, they were on the road, and we were in front of the TV watching the pre-game programming from the Monday Night broadcast team. We were glued to the screen right up until halftime. Then I had an idea.

"Charlie, why don't we stay up and watch the halftime highlights with Howard Cosell, and then go to bed?"

He nodded. I knew he would. Before long, halftime highlights led right into the first series of the second half. Then there was touchdown after touchdown! Before we knew it, the game reached its exciting conclusion when Mark Moseley of the Skins missed a field goal

"Whoa! All right! " I hollered as Charlie and I high-five'd each other.

When we realized how late it was, it instantly hit us. We were in for big trouble.

"Oh, man. What are we gonna tell Mom and Dad?" Both of our brains started frantically whirling to come up with a plausible excuse. We sure weren't perfect kids, but we were honest enough with ourselves to know we needed to 'come clean' on this one.

Then, just as quickly, what surfaced was a new realization that with traffic jams and travel time, our parents wouldn't be home for an hour or more. It wasn't until years later that I admitted to our dad that we had stayed up to watch the whole game.

"I would have, too," he chuckled.

I can't help but wonder if my sons will do something similar someday. I hope I'd be just as gracious as my dad was when I say to them, "Okay, maybe this one time, just like Dad and Uncle Charlie did on October 17, 1983!"

By Cary Mares

CR ED

50 Lance Has the Packers Covered

Growing up in Rice Lake, WI…I lived and died by what happened with the Packers on Sunday afternoons, and mostly died. You see, I was born in 1970. After the Lombardi era Packers, I knew the history of Titletown, and the legacy of the Packers, but rarely during those times did I see it. There was an 8-7-1 season in 1978 then a refreshing playoff appearance in 1982. And some of the record-setting performances of 1983 were all I knew. I still remember one of my favorite memories was watching games with my grandfather. He'd get so angry at the Packers and yell at the TV.

"You guys couldn't tackle or beat the Weirgor Wildcats!" he'd shout.

By the way, Weirgor is a town with a population of 100 max. Saaalute!" The difficult and challenging times as I was growing up didn't diminish my love of the Pack. I still remember going to my first game. I recall going to the Packers Hall of Fame for the first time. I spotted Tony Mandarich at the Denny's on Oneida Street, the Sunday morning before the season's first game against Tampa Bay. He'd just signed his contract, but wasn't going to play in that game.

"Tony, uh, could I get your autograph?"

"Sure," he told me.

Wow, he was big. I remember another game in 1985, the Snow Bowl in Lambeau Field against the Buccaneers, when Steve Young didn't know what hit him, between the snow and Alphonso Carreker (a Packers lineman who sacked him stuffing his facemask into the snow). I listened to that game while deer hunting and then struggled home as the Packers struggled through the drifts and won 23-0.

I am one of many sportscasters who've had to move away from home to follow their dreams and I hope someday I can move back. I went to college at UW-Madison. I was able to start my TV career in Rhinelander, WI, and then continue it in Green Bay and Milwaukee. I've covered the teams I grew up with for 18 years…something I'll never take for granted. It has truly been and continues to be an honor to cover the team I have grown up with, the Green Bay Packers.

By Lance Allan, WTMJ-TV4, Milwaukee

ଔ ଛ

51 Omar Gets Another Chance

Don and Marion Koepke founded a program called Another Chance, Inc. Being foster parents themselves, they recognized a gap existed between foster care, juvenile justice and jail or prison. Another Chance filled that gap by placing young people in 24/7 mentoring care with volunteer "parents." Omar was one of the young men in the program who was living with them while attending Oshkosh University. He came into the Another Chance program from Rawhide Boys Ranch, a part of Wisconsin's juvenile justice system. Omar was a hard worker with an active faith in God. He did, however, have one big flaw. He was a Dallas Cowboy fan.

One day the Koepkes and Omar were invited to Rawhide to hear Reggie White speak. The great #92 Packer defensive end gave an inspiring talk to the young men in the audience. He told them that what first and foremost led to real success was to love God and to follow Christ. Reggie went on to encourage them to recognize that, while they may have a past which included some terrible things like assaults, dysfunctional families, gangs and/or drugs, from this point forward they needed to put all excuses behind them and take full responsibility for their actions. He went on to acknowledge that Rawhide can give them a huge helping hand, but, in the final analysis, it would come down to the choices each person makes. Good choices, or bad ones, each will determine the path of their lives.

As Reggie was signing autographs afterward, 5'3" Omar, flaunting a Dallas Cowboy shirt, walked up to 6'6" Reggie with just four words for the Packer great.

"You ain't so tough!"

Reggie picked Omar up off the ground, looked him square in the eyes and said "Oh, Yeah!?"

They both started laughing. On that day, a Dallas Cowboy fan became a Packer fan, or at least a fan of one Packer in particular...another great example of God's power (or man's brute strength) to set a wayward soul on the right path.

By Marion Koepke

CR 80

Omar with Reggie White

52 Kathy's Answered Prayer

WEMI, my favorite Christian radio station, was having their yearly spring fundraiser. It was May of 2004. I sensed I was to make a contribution on the first day, but didn't have time to call. On the second day, I felt that same urge to pledge $100, but, again, I didn't find the time to call. On the third and final day while listening to the station on my drive in to work, I listened as another woman called in.

She confessed to the listeners that for the last two days she felt the need to call in a pledge, but hadn't done so. Now, she knew she had to do it today. I knew instantly that this was my cue, so I pulled to the side of the road and dialed.

"Hi, WEMI Share-a-thon," someone answered.

"Yes, my name is Kathy Lorenz. I'd like to make a pledge of $100," I offered.

The woman on the other end chatted with me for several minutes. I found myself divulging a variety of facts about my life. I told her I was recently married to Ed, that I lived in Chilton, WI, and we attended Faith Alliance Church. I hung up the phone, confident I had done the right thing.

As I continued my drive to work, an important and exciting announcement caught my attention. I knew Ed would want to know about this, as well. I turned up the volume so I wouldn't miss a single detail.

"We've had a generous donor give us two Packer tickets. We'll be giving them away in a drawing to someone who made a pledge this morning."

I smiled, and wondered if it perhaps wasn't providential that I had waited to pledge. The announcer continued.

"The tickets are for the Monday night game on October 4 when the Packers will be taking on the Tennessee Titans. So, if you were one of the fortunate ones who had pledged between 7 and 8 this morning, you may be headed to a Packer game."

As I continued my drive to work I whispered a little prayer.

"Dear God, I know You love me. I know You asked me to make a contribution and I did. You know that I'll love You no matter what, but

I'd sure love to win the tickets!"

I smiled to myself. "Now, how could God ignore a prayer like that?"

Once I arrived at work, I took a few minutes to tell my daughter that I was in the running for two Packer tickets, that the drawing was going to be held at 9:30 that morning, and that I had asked God to bless me with the tickets. We laughed about it, but I couldn't help but feel God was going to answer my prayer. Ask and you shall receive, right?

I was driving to the post office to pick up the office mail, still tuned in to WEMI, when I heard the announcer declare they had just drawn the name of the person who had won the tickets.

"The winner of the Packer tickets is a lady who told us she had recently married Ed and they live in Chilton."

I had won! I hollered, cried and thanked God all at the same time. I was ecstatic. What a Godincidence! When I returned to work, I told everyone I had won the tickets. Then I called the radio station and told them the story, too.

Ed and I went to that Monday night game. It was a great night at Lambeau Field even though the Packers lost. I didn't mind, really. I was still marveling at my answered prayer.

By the way, can you guess how much the face value of the tickets was? They were worth $100.

God has such a great sense of humor!

By Kathy Lorenz

CR SO

53 There's Nobody Like the Packers

I was born in Ohio, but later lived in Texas for 27 years. I followed the Dallas Cowboys during the Roger Staubach era, and was good friends with Preston Pearson's kids who lived right down the street from me.

Living in Dallas was quite different than living in Ohio. Everything was about the 'big' factor: big houses, big city, and big trucks. Even the hair was big! Being a Cowboy fan was big, too. I watched the Cowboys at every opportunity. I loved Charlie Waters, Tony Dorsett and, most of all, Roger Staubach. I was totally enamored with them. From my perspective, the Cowboys epitomized what professional football was all about, particularly at that time in my life.

Within a few years of graduating from high school in 1985, two things happened. First, in 1989, I married my lovely wife Cheryl who's from Appleton, WI. Second, Jerry Jones acquired the Cowboys. My football world fell apart. Although my hope was that everything would remain as it was, and they would still be the Cowboys that I grew up with, it was not to be.

Around this same time my wife asked if I would watch the Packer games with her. I thought it couldn't hurt. After all, I had visited the great white north and had been exposed to the awesome force that is known as "Packermania," so why not? I freely admit it. I got hooked! The primary reason for my new-found addiction was the novel idea of a team that was not only owned by the fans, but positively adored by their fans, not to mention that the Packers were one of the teams to actually start the NFL.

In my opinion, the piece de resistance came in 1992, when Brett Favre was acquired from Atlanta. I couldn't get enough of the Packers. I was beginning to realize what so many around the world already were aware of, that the Packers are a very special team, and that Green Bay is a special town. I found myself eagerly anticipating Sunday and Packer games. I proudly drove my truck around in Cowboy territory brandishing a big Green Bay magnet on the tailgate. Not once did any of the loyal Cowboy fans accost me. Maybe they knew better.

Or maybe it was because there was a certain level of respect for Green Bay. No one would argue that the Packers were a formidable team in the making and were on the road to even more greatness than they had already achieved. Green Bay, from the smallest market in the NFL, is able to play and beat teams from larger markets. Now, that's moxie!

It's no secret that the Green Bay Packers have devoted fans everywhere, including Dallas, TX. There are a number of Packer bars in Dallas where the faithful gather to support their team. I know, because my family and I had frequented them from time to time.

Today, I live in the state of Wisconsin. I so enjoy the fact that I am now a bona fide member of "Packermania." I've also had the pleasure of going to a Packer game at Lambeau Field during the winter. Without question, the most striking aspect of that game was the fact that it was in the high 20s and every seat in the house was filled, bar none. I am utterly convinced that there could have been a blizzard and the result would have been the same. There are no fair weather fans in Green Bay. Through thick and thin, we stand our ground and watch our boys play their hearts out. This is yet another reason I love being a Packer fan. There's no other team like them.

The moral of this story is that I have discovered a real team, with real history, and real fans. How could I do anything but become one myself? I will be forever and a day, through thick and thin, a dyed-in-the-soul green and gold fanatic.

I was a Cowboy fan, but I have come to my senses. It definitely is better late than never, right?

By Michael Woerner

CR SO

54 The Packer Rock

It's really not important that he's an award-winning broadcaster who knows more about football than most people could forget. It's not important that he can say more about a football play in three words than a person could say in two sentences. What is important is that former Green Bay Packer player Larry McCarren is a true gentleman, who has a wonderful way with people, and whose word is as good as gold.

Whether he's in character with his macho edginess as he hosts Larry's Locker Room TV program, which runs during the football season, or he's the colorful analyst alongside Packer play-by-play man Wayne Larrivee on the Green Bay Packers Radio Network, underneath the professional presentation is a kind and laid-back role model.

Larry "The Rock" McCarren was born in Park Forest, IL, in 1951, and was actually a Bears fan, although he didn't despise the NFC Central opponent to the north.

"I didn't hate the Packers, not by any means. I even read Jerry Kramer's *Distant Replay*," he recalled.

Larry would learn to love the Packers, the team, the town, and the tradition after being drafted in the 12th round in 1973 by Green Bay out of the University of Illinois. He played until 1984, a very solid and durable center, making 162 consecutive starts, the fourth highest record in team history. Thus, his nickname, "The Rock." He was selected to play in two Pro Bowls in '82 and '83. He was inducted into the Green Bay Packer Hall of Fame in 1992. He has gone on to garner numerous Wisconsin Broadcaster of the Year awards. Larry, however, is not about the glitz or the accolades.

After his playing days were over, Larry stayed in Green Bay. He got into the business world for a few years at Bellin Hospital before landing in TV. Today, his day-to-day 365-days-a-year job is as the Sports Director for WFRV-TV 5.

"When Larry came to audition for the TV sports job, we knew he didn't have any experience. But we said, 'Hey, if he works half as hard at this job as he did on the field, this will be a winning decision,'" remembers Perry Kidder, the General Manager.

The rest, as they say, is history. Larry not only landed that job, but teamed with Jim Irwin and Max McGee in 1995, and has been in the booth with Wayne Larrivee since 1999.

The TV and radio gigs don't have the spotlights or the glamour that come when you play pro ball in front of 70,000 people 16 times a year. The gigs don't offer the hundreds of thousands of dollars per year either, but Larry is happy and healthy, and most of all grateful.

As for the money aspect, he did make hundreds of thousands per year, not the millions that players today make. When asked if he felt any animosity for helping to pave the way for players to make millions shortly after his playing days were over, he had no complaints.

"Not in the least. No matter what era you played in, you were well paid. It was a great ride. We made executive-type salaries and it was a privilege to play in the National Football League, much less for the Green Bay Packers. It doesn't get any better than that," professed McCarren.

One of Larry's practices was to get out on Lambeau Field early on game day to a special section where people in wheelchairs or people with special friends representing important causes were seated.

"I always wanted to thank them for coming to the game."

Larry has the usual great things to say about the team, the town and the fans. He holds the same opinion as many do, that former president and CEO Bob Harlan may be the nicest man on the earth. Larry, however, took it a step further.

"Not only was he a great guy, but he was an effective leader. That's not easy to do," the Rock pointed out.

Larry's colleagues have nothing but great things to say about him. More than once, someone has overheard Larry telling young camera people to make sure they have designated drivers, and he's been seen, on a number of occasions, pulling cash from his wallet just in case they needed cab fare.

One of Larry's passions is airplanes. He's been a licensed pilot for years. His partner in the radio play-by-play booth, Wayne Larrivee, has high praise for his friend, as well.

"Larry's a no-fluff guy. We don't spend a lot of time talking about the family before broadcasts. He's a professional who's great to work with. When we go out on the road, we don't go to fancy restaurants. We both like to just sit at the bar with a burger and watch a game on TV," Larrivee gave as an inside note.

"There was one time when bad weather was going to keep me from making it to the next place where I needed to do a broadcast, so Larry

Dave Rose and Larry McCarren

flew down, picked me up, and got me to the next city. When Larry says something, his word is good. He'll be there for you. He's certainly been there for me. He's a great broadcaster, no doubt about it, and an even better friend," Larrivee continued.

This writer would like to share that when our first book came out in '96, Larry was the first broadcaster to do a radio interview. At the time, he and Green Bay radio personality John Miano were doing a show together. They were both great to me. Larry is a straight shooter, for sure, but he's also a genuinely nice guy.

I mentioned to Larry during my interview for this chapter, that I'd get him a copy of this story for his approval.

"Steve, you know what you're doing. I trust you. Just write your book."

Thank you, my friend. I took you up on that offer, so I can only hope you're okay with people knowing that underneath that gruff, macho exterior beats the heart of a kind, soft-hearted man, and one who many in the Green Bay community are proud to know.

By Steve Rose with memories from Larry McCarren

CR SO

55 It's Only a Game

Mike Hunt wore #55 when he played for the Packers from 1978 to 1980. He appeared in only 22 games, a short career by most standards. That may be one reason he espouses to the theory that football is "only a game," but there's an even more compelling reason.

Hunt moved with his family as a 15-year-old from Casper, WY, to Ortonville, MN, in 1972. His dad was a Packer fan, clearly an intelligent man!

"He used to have Coke bottle caps with the players' names on the inside of them. I wish I still had them. I wonder what they'd be worth?"

With three younger brothers and a sister, Mike's job was to fish, hunt and grow a vegetable garden to help feed the family. The solidly-built gentleman didn't start playing football until his sophomore year in high school, but he caught on quickly and soon found himself drafted out of the University of Minnesota in the 2nd round by the Packers. Mike had some great moments and potential, but headaches and a flickering in his left eye caused by concussions forced him to hang up his spikes in '80 to avoid the risk of further, more permanent, injury.

I met Mike many years ago. At the time, he and his brother Fred were running a hardware store in Menasha, WI. It's always fun to meet either former or current players, but there's something special about Mike. I've met some tender hearts off the field, but none like Mike Hunt. He showed me some of his memorabilia in a rather nonchalant sort of way. I suspect he would have never done it without my prompting.

"Here's a game ball, Steve, that I got when we beat the Patriots on Monday Night Football in 1979," he said.

"Mike, I remember that game well. My friend Jim Zielinski from Menasha and I watched that game at his place. David Whitehurst was the quarterback, right?"

"He was," he acknowledged, somewhat surprised that I would remember.

"What are a few of your favorite memories or memorable moments on the field," I asked as he leaned his elbows on the counter.

"I remember the first time I tackled Walter Payton, I landed right on top of him at the end of the play."

"Good hit, man!" Payton told me as we got up.

"I had many chances to tackle him, but it usually ended up that I barely got my hand on him, or I missed him all together. One time, during my rookie season, I missed a tackle right on the Packer sidelines. As I got up to go back to the huddle, I heard someone call my name. Then he started yelling at me. I looked back to see none other than Ray Nitschke himself, and he was mad!" smiled Mike.

Today, Mike lives in Merrill, WI, just a few hours northwest of Green Bay.

"After traveling all around the country while playing for the Packers, I can honestly say there's no place more beautiful than northeast Wisconsin. There's no better place to live, no better people, no better fans, no better team. I am and always will be a Packer fan."

Mike Hunt has always been a gentle giant with a good soul, but I'm sure that his character became even more refined when he got the devastating news that his son, Isaiah, died on Nov 15, 2004, in Baghdad, Iraq. Isaiah was only 20 years old.

Isaiah was in the 82nd Airborne, stationed at Ft. Bragg, NC, before his deployment. Pam, Isaiah's mom, and Mike attended the Memorial Day service there in 2005. Mike and Pam met President George W. Bush and spent nearly 15 minutes visiting with him. The president made an intelligent observation as he eyed up Mike.

"You look like you could have played for the Packers."

"Yes, sir. I did," Mike affirmed.

"I gave the president a pin with Isaiah's picture on it and he sent me a letter a couple of weeks later informing me that he would be putting the pin in his library. I want to get down there to see it someday," he continued, his eyes staring off in the distance.

There is another memory that's close to Mike's heart.

"The preseason Charger game at Lambeau Field in 2005 was an exciting event for us. Four of Isaiah's Army buddies, who had been with him the night he died, called us to ask if they could come up to watch a Packer game with us. We got it lined up, had the tickets, everything was set. Then we got a call from a friend of the Favres inviting us all to watch the game from Brett's private box. Needless to say, we weren't about to turn down an offer like that. After the game, Brett's mom came over to talk with us."

"Would you boys like to go down and meet Brett when he comes out of the locker room?" she asked.

"We didn't turn down that offer, either," Mike remembers fondly.

For Mike Hunt, the Green Bay Packers will always be special, but at the end of the day, don't fault him for his belief that, in the bigger scheme of things, "it's only a game."

In Memoriam to Isaiah R. Hunt, who is buried at the St. Edward & Isadore Church Cemetery in Suamico, WI.

By Steve Rose with memories from Mike Hunt

56 Jammin' With Nick Five-Six

☙ ❧

I've been in radio for over 17 years. For me, the most stressful thing I do is to put on concerts for our listeners. There are just too many variables that I can't control. Will enough people show up? Do we have the equipment/security/prizes/banners/etc.? Will the artists arrive on time? How will our celebrity host act when on stage?

On December 18, 2009, those last two questions played a huge role in how my evening would end up! The night started out great. Our 95.9 KISS FM staff was in rare form. Everyone was doing his part. Banners were hung; interviewees interviewed; the first two acts had sound checked and were back at the hotel. When the doors opened, the room at *Tom, Dick and Harry's* filled up the room nicely.

Doug and Mary, our morning team, got up in front of the throng of listeners, welcomed them, and then introduced our celebrity host, Green Bay Packer linebacker Nick Barnett. The crowd went wild. The night was definitely off to a great start.

Act one: Bee Scott, an artist on Nick Barnett's Clarity Music Group label, did a phenomenal job. Act two: Kristinia DeBarge, daughter of one of the original DeBarges, was fantastic. She was with some of the best dancers I've ever seen flying all over the stage. The crowd loved it, and so did I, or at least I should have.

Unfortunately, I was backstage making phone calls to band managers, limo companies and the hotel trying to locate our final act. Kristinia's set ended altogether too soon (or so it seemed). Meanwhile, I was backstage conjuring up ideas of how to fill an hour before our final act made it to the venue. Luckily for me, I didn't have to fill anything.

Packer linebacker and great personality Nick Barnett (56) jumped on stage and instantly had our listeners eating out of his hand. He spent the next hour rapping with his artist Bee, hosting a dance-off on stage, and actually was able to get Kristinia's dancers back up for another few moves. Frankly, he was doing anything and everything to keep the masses entertained.

I've never seen a man work the crowd as hard (or as well) as Nick did. This guy not only knew how to entertain us on the football field, he knew how to entertain, period. Our third act finally arrived and took the stage.

Dayton Kane with Nick Barnett

Nick walked off, sweat

pouring from his forehead and massive arms, and sat down in the wings. The only thing he asked for was water. Nicely played.

By Dayton Kane

ભ ૹ

57 $18 Bought Us a Good Super Bowl

After Green Bay was victorious in the Ice Bowl, several friends and I began talking about going to Miami for Super Bowl II. We had all watched the first Super Bowl and now, with what seemed to be the imminent return of the Packers it became a real possibility that history would repeat itself. Needless to say, the idea of leaving the frozen tundra of the North for the sunny beaches of South Florida seemed like a no brainer. Admittedly, we were young, naïve in some ways, and probably even a bit foolish back then, just four single guys, each in our early twenties, who grew up only 40 miles from Green Bay, aka. Titletown, which we believed was the football capital of the world (or, of our world, at the very least).

With only two weeks to get to the game itself, there was not a lot of time to make arrangements with our employers, come up with the money, make motel reservations, or get tickets to the game. No matter that the last two weren't actually nailed down. Full of optimism, we were finally on our way in the middle of the final week before the game. Since I had the newest car, a '67 Pontiac Le Mans, it was requisitioned for the 1,100-mile trip south to Fort Lauderdale, FL.

We took turns driving, finally arriving tired and weary, twenty-two hours later. We lucked out in finding one motel, the Merriweather, which still had a room available. This would now become our temporary shelter from wintery Wisconsin, and our base from which to search out the area beaches and nightlife. Did I mention we still needed to find tickets to the game?

There was incredible excitement in the balmy Fort Lauderdale air.

Football fans from all over the country gathered to celebrate the matchup between the Packers and the AFL Champion Oakland Raiders. We seemed to be the only ones who spent at least a few hours each day soaking up the sun by the pool.

Evening, however, was quite a different story. Folks seemed to come out of the woodwork. Local restaurants and nightclubs were standing room only. Two nights before the game, we were able to purchase four tickets. If memory serves me well, we had to pay an additional $10 scalping fee, which brought each ticket up to the lofty price of $18.

Speaking of nightclubs, amazingly, the night before the game, we found ourselves sitting at the same table with two of the Packer running backs, Donny Anderson and Chuck Mercein. As I recall, they both were very gracious and quite friendly. In fact, Anderson knew one of the fellows I was with as he was the company clerk who had signed up Donny Anderson and Jim Grabowski for the Oshkosh National Guard Unit. It never hurts to have connections.

The final leg of our most excellent adventure was when we arrived at the Orange Bowl in Miami on game day, January 14, 1968. The temperature was in the high sixties with plenty of sunshine. We were seated in a corner of the Raiders end zone. There were two plays that still stand out to me today.

The first was an opening running play by Oakland, when a Packer middle linebacker met the ball carrier as he came through the line and flipped him head over heels. The Packer fans really came alive with that hit. Although the play was on the opposite end of the field, we could easily see the dramatic result of the collision. Then I heard a comment I will never forget.

"That had to have been Nitschke who made that tackle."

It was.

The second most memorable play happened in the second period. Bart Starr caught the Raider defensive off guard with a 62-yard play action pass to Boyd Dowler, who then ran the ball right into the corner of our end zone for a touchdown. The Packers were never behind and went on to win their second Super Bowl in a row, 34 to 14.

Packers–Two. AFL–Zero.

Perhaps the most significant moment, however, occurred after the victory. Little did any of us know that when the team carried Vince

Lombardi off the field, it would be his last game as head coach of the Packers. And none of us would have ever imagined that when we began our journey to watch our heroes.

By Pastor Dan Kiefer

CR ∽Ɔ

58 Hey, Who You Kicking Out?

As someone in the "50-plus category," I've been blessed to have lived through two great periods of Packer football history, the first being the glory years of the '60s and the second being the Holmgren/Favre era. During the latter period, I had the privilege of twiddling the knobs and switches as engineer for Steve Rose's Leap of Faith radio program, a 30-minute look at faith and Packer football that aired on 12 Midwest radio affiliates during the '96-'97 and '97-'98 seasons.

Recognizing that God has important work planned in advance for each member of His kingdom, it didn't matter if the guest was a "stop gap" player like Paul Frase or one of those who are now Packer legends like Robert Brooks and Don Beebe. The message of salvation through Christ and living His principles remained the same.

As for humorous experiences, two in particular stand out. The first was an ongoing source of entertainment, and the second one I can now laugh about only because I managed to avoid bringing a massive amount of embarrassment to both Steve and me!

John Michels, Steve's co-host, was a young left tackle from USC drafted by the Packers in the first round in 1996. The Packers were looking to him to be a future offensive line star. Talented as he was, the team thought he was too light and needed to put on weight...lots of it. That's not an unusual situation for players making the transition to the pro game, but to watch the player in question actually working at the solution was quite a sight.

You see, John would regularly show up with a number of fast-food bags and Steve and I would have to wait until he was finished "bulking up" before we could begin recording. It became a point of amazement and humor for me and Steve. In fact, if John were in his 20's today, he'd make an excellent spokesperson for Hardees; a real anti-Jared because there's no way Subway's Jared Fogle could bear to watch how much fast food John consumed. And according to Steve's journal notes, this was between lunch and dinner! Talk about a dream diet!

Then came my "don't judge a book by its cover" moment. I also learned that even if you're a "behind the scenes" employee as I was, in sports broadcasting it really does pay to carefully study the media guide. Young, budding sports broadcasters, take note. We were very much at the mercy of John in terms of the names and number of the individuals who would be appearing on the program. Steve was fine with that given that he was a real pro at asking the right questions without having to engage in a lot of pre-show preparation.

One taping day I noticed a 20-something, non-football looking character hanging around the studio talking to a female employee from the local Christian radio station located in the same building. Was he a friend of hers, or a fellow employee from the radio station, or was he waiting around for the guest(s) to arrive so that he could get a quick autograph? That autograph issue was something Steve and I wanted to handle carefully because we didn't want the players to feel like the show was an autograph trap.

Like most people, I'm not very comfortable with confrontations, but as our recording deadline loomed I was getting annoyed. This fellow didn't seem to be in any hurry to leave. Just about the time I was gathering up the nerve to approach this guy to ask him to politely "hit the dusty trail," I decided I'd better ask someone else who he was. It was a good thing I did. I would have made a complete fool of myself attempting to "kick out" the man who would become one of the most prolific field goal kickers in Packer history.

Who was the boyish looking guy wearing glasses and a baseball cap? None other than Ryan Longwell, the guest John had brought in for the show!

By Bob Gardinier

CR ♌

59 The Packers Dare to Be Great

Touchdown!!! These are words every football fan loves to hear unless, of course, you're on the wrong side of that equation. Growing up in Benton, MS, as a New Orleans Saints fan, I seldom had much to cheer about. Sure, it's easy to admit you're a Saints fan after they win the Super Bowl, but I was a fan of Archie Manning, Bobby Hebert, and the Awesome Foursome of Sam Mills, Vaughn Johnson, Ricky Jackson, and Pat Swilling.

I wasn't exposed all that much to the Green Bay Packers until 1993 when they signed Reggie White. That was the beginning of unrestricted free agency in the NFL and the big splash for the Packers was Reggie. The few Packer friends I had were already beginning to have Super Bowl aspirations. I thought it was silly at the time, but I willingly admit my admiration of their loyalty and dedication to their team. In fact, one of the things I most admired about the Packers and the organization was their proud history and tradition of winning in the smallest professional sports market.

In 1996, I moved to the heart of Packer country and almost immediately was swept up into Packermania. What I've discovered since living in the Fox Valley area is that the Packer organization, players, and leaders in the front office are individuals who dare to be great. I believe that at the heart of every man lies a hidden desire to rise above the natural boundaries and take that one shot at greatness. To dare to be great can have natural and sometimes unintended consequences. Every true pioneer faces the potential for danger on the horizon of new or unexplored frontiers.

Greatness is not something that comes without great sacrifice and commitment. These are qualities I have noticed are abundant in Green Bay. Football is a great sport and many an athlete has pursued his dream of making it to the NFL, but never got there. For those precious few individuals who hear their name called out on draft day, it's the culmination of years of hard work, blood, sweat, and tears. Their reward is that ultimate stage of battle where greatness is measured in inches at a time, and the margin for error is slim.

The Green Bay Packers have a proud history and tradition of winning. Their fans are arguably the best, and they back it up with sellout after sellout, regardless of either current or past records. I am, admittedly, a huge Brett Favre fan. I watched him in person play for USM and followed his career closely. The decision to retire, or not retire, became a long and often times painful process. It became the butt of jokes and the subject of many a talk-radio show and late-night comedian.

Brett is a great quarterback, so when he left Green Bay many thought that the demise of the Packers was imminent. Daring to be great begins with one simple principle, risk. You can't aspire to greatness if all you pursue is the safety of the known. The Green Bay Packers allowed Brett to leave, and took a risk on a relatively new hotshot named Aaron Rogers.

I was sad to see Brett go, no doubt about it, but I confess that my respect for the Packer organization grew during the ensuing weeks and months. It's not easy to say goodbye to a legend. I don't know what kind of career Aaron Rogers will or won't have, but he's taken the reigns of the team and has continued the tradition of success the Packers have established.

This would not have happened were it not for more than a few people who were willing to take a risk. Any dare-to-be great opportunity begins with risk, and that is one quality that never seems to be in short supply in Green Bay.

But there's another component to greatness that seldom gets discussed. It's the idea that we each are a part of something bigger than our individual selves. That "something" is called community.

If you've never been to a Green Bay Packers practice, then you've missed one of the finest examples of community. Thousands of fans show up every year to watch the team practice. They cheer and watch with eager anticipation, knowing everything that's happening on the practice field has potential for success across the street at legendary Lambeau Field.

Lombardi knew that success for his team was also linked to an understanding of community. He embraced that, and started a tradition that no other NFL franchise has. Lombardi allowed his players to ride kids' bikes to and from the practice field. The same kids who came to watch the practices would lend their wheels to Packer players. Sometimes the players hitched a ride on the back of the bike while the kids pedaled furiously to help the player reach his destination. Other times players "borrowed" the bikes and rode them while the owner proudly ran beside the bike. That same tradition is carried on yet today. If you play for the Packers, you join a family, not just a team.

On Sundays, 53 men proudly wear the Packer uniform and go into battle, but they do not go alone. They have an entire family, a community, who stands in the trenches with them.

Greatness starts with an individual or a team taking a risk and taking that risk means growing into a community. The Packer organization and its players embrace the community to which they belong. That's what makes them a model of success in this ever-competitive world.

If you've never been to a Packer practice, make your plans now to do so. You won't be disappointed.

By Wes Powell

ರ ಬಿ

60 The Voice Inside Lambeau

If you've been to a Packer game anytime since 2005, the voice you've heard commentating such plays as, "Tackle by Nick Barnett and Ryan Pickett," is that of Bill Jartz. Bill's day job is as a prominent news anchor for WBAY-TV 2 in Green Bay. It's been an exciting ride for Bill up to the Lambeau Field Press Box.

His friends, and I am proud to be one of them, call him "Jartzy." Bill, by most standards, could easily be one who is considered to have "made it" in Green Bay. Success, however, has not altered the fact that he's a gracious, kind man who loves to laugh and does so often. Bill's childhood was spent within an hour's drive from Green Bay in the small town of Clintonville. He grew up, like many of us, watching the Dick Rodgers Polka show before kickoff. Here's a fact that might surprise you.

"My father wasn't much of a Packer fan, so if we wanted to watch the game, we'd have to go over to our friends' houses to watch it," he remembers.

What did the teenage Jartz think were some of the coolest things about the Packers?

"I thought the 'G' on the helmet was very cool. By the time I started faithfully watching the Packers, I was so committed to them, I refused to believe anything other than the fact that they were going to win every time they got on the field," he pointed out.

Bill, himself, was no slouch on the field, having earned a scholarship to be an offensive lineman at the Northwestern University in Chicago. Ironically, it was there he may have been bitten by the broadcast bug.

"My roommate's dad, Walt Versen, was on the stats crew for the Chicago Bears. That gave us access to the press box at Soldier Field. I was mesmerized by the whole experience. Looking back, I'm sure it played a significant role in what I do today."

During his college-year summers, Bill worked in construction. He was often recruited by his boss to drive into Green Bay for supplies, taking him past the Green Bay practice field. He never imagined he would eventually have a TV broadcast career, much less that he'd be working with the Green Bay Packers in the public address capacity.

Bill planted his first professional seeds at Channel 7 WSAW in Wausau before coming to Green Bay. One of his first green and gold memories was a press conference with Bart Starr.

"Bart recognized that I was the new kid on the block. He came up to me afterward and said 'Welcome to Green Bay.' I'll never forget that," recounts Jartz.

In 2005, Gary Knafelc, who'd been doing the public address for the Packers for many years, retired. It was then that Jartz got the call of a lifetime.

"The Packers called to let me know they wanted me for the job. They thought I was the guy, but they wanted me to audition. I called my spotter, Andy Thompson, with whom I had worked when I did preseason games for WBAY, and asked him to come up and help. We were also high school teammates on the Truckers' offensive line."

A nervous Jartz made his way up to the 7th floor inside Lambeau Field to the booth in the southwest end zone of Lambeau Field! The heat was really on when he was given instructions as to how to operate the speaker box.

"Let's have you do a starting lineup," they requested.

"I remember Bob Harlan was down on the field, and I was shaking like a leaf on a windy day. I took a deep breath, got my composure, and began," Bill admits with a chuckle.

"And at quarterback, from the University of Southern Mississippi…#4 Brett Favre!" he projected over the empty stadium.

Something else memorable happened that day, as well.

"There was a tour going on inside the stadium, so here's this group of people wondering what was going on as I'm giving the starting lineups. I wondered if they actually expected to see Brett come running out on the field," said Bill with a deep, hearty laugh.

Bill's day job is with the TV station, but it's no surprise that most people want to talk to him about his work on eight Sundays a year with the Packers. It's clear he's working his dream job at the house that Curly Lambeau built.

"It's so exciting. Everyone in the booth is pumped. The crowd is electrified. Then Mike McKenna says, 'Billy, bring them out!'"

Does it get any better than that? We might be tempted to think that the only ones who are living their dreams are the ones on the field. Not so. Look up into the booth and you'll see the boy who's done very well for himself.

Better yet, close your eyes and listen to the voice say, "Rodgers, 18-yards to Driver, and it's a touchdown!"

By Steve Rose with memories from Bill Jartz
WBAY TV-2, Public Address, Green Bay Packers

❧ ❦

61 Let Me Say This

I came to Wisconsin in the summer of 1975, having moved from eastern Ohio. I followed pro football during the season, but would move on to baseball and other things as the calendar pages turned. I especially liked the Pittsburgh Steelers.

My wife and I had been told, or perhaps warned would be more accurate, to expect a couple of things in Wisconsin. First, it stays at least thirty below zero all winter long. Second, the locals take their Green Bay Packers very seriously. The first was obviously a gross exaggeration, but that second one had something to it.

Our first December here, I remember two women in my office shedding tears of joy when, on Christmas Eve, the fabled Bart Starr was named the new Packer coach. The fair-haired hero of the Lombardi era signed on to right the sinking ship that had sprung several leaks under Dan Devine. Even though the champagne flowed, albeit briefly, and the fans hoped, the green and gold continued to flop under Starr, Gregg, and Infante. The coaching was weak, the talent even weaker. Where was the storied franchise headed? Though the floundering continued, the fans remained rabid.

Enter Ron Wolf and Mike Holmgren. In 1992, GM Wolf swung the deal trading for the barely-known and relatively green Brett Favre. The guy was a good-ole-boy gunslinger from Mississippi. He threw the ball often and hard, and sometimes to the opponents. Watching him could be agonizing and frustrating, to say the least, but his love for the game and the fun he was having was unsurpassed. The fans were reinvigorated. His reputation for generating excitement, and his talent of making something out of nothing was pure joy to watch. Surround him with a few more players and get a couple of years of experience and he, in the words of more than a few, would lead us to the Promised Land.

More talent was added to the roster with Reggie, Desmond and a few others, and the Super Bowl trophy found its way back to Green Bay. Happy days were here again, and Brett could do no wrong. This seemed like it could go on forever! The crazy fans went even crazier.

Coaching and personnel changed. The aging factor and injuries came to the fore of conversation, to say nothing of some terrible draft choices. The natives got restless. And Ted Thompson? He got even more restless. He seemed to be thinking the unthinkable - it may be time for Brett to go. He had drafted a young kid from California and he wanted him to play.

All hell broke loose. Brett was taking too long to contemplate retirement. TT was irked. Maybe Brett could be a backup because Mr. Rodgers was now the golden child.

So, Brett ended up with the Jets. Gone. Just like that. The entire fiasco was poorly conceived, poorly handled and even more poorly explained, but what do I know? The Packers, it seemed, dumped their hero, but they wouldn't allow him to stay in their division. A good question to ask might have been, "If Ted Thompson thought he was over the hill, then who cares where he goes?"

Enter the Vikings, in need of a good quarterback. Brett would now be wearing purple and gold and would become a part of the evil empire, the dark force. Some Packer fans reacted as they should, wished Brett well and even cheered him on. Far too many, however, had another curious reaction, hoping he would play poorly or get hurt. It was a bit obscene, in my opinion.

The gunslinger was still being a gunslinger and loving every minute of it. He led the Vikings to the 2010 NFC championship game to go head to head with Drew Brees. In short, Brett just kept being Brett.

I still follow the Steelers, though I have developed some interest in the Packers. None the less, I still have difficulty trying to determine why so many green and gold fans and the Packer brass turned against Favre.

In the spirit of good sportsmanship, let's give Brett his due. Even as his luster dims, it's difficult not to remember all the thrills he's brought to football fans. Watch the highlight reels of 16 great years in Green Bay. And don't be surprised if, in a few years, he's holding a bust of himself in Canton.

Thanks, Brett.

By David White

CR SO

62 Marco Left His Heart in Green Bay

Marco Rivera learned quite a few things while working in Green Bay from 1996 to 2004. He learned that Green Bay, the organization, and the team are great, and the fans supporting them are the best in the world.

While growing up in Brooklyn, Marco understandably had a dream to play for the New York Giants after being a fan of Coach Bill Parcells and quarterback Phil Simms. But he will tell you those desires evaporated like Wisconsin's April snow when he got drafted by the Packers in the 6th round in 1996.

"Suddenly, I found myself playing with Reggie White and Keith Jackson. I had admired both of them so much when I was growing up. I was playing against Bruce Smith and other great players, but with Reggie and Keith on your side, you knew you were going to be okay," recalled Rivera.

Marco admitted that White was the one who had the biggest impact on him.

"I watched the way he conducted himself in the locker room. His leadership and presence was so great. Brett was the one to get all the records, but Reggie was the one who had everyone's attention. He was such a great role model for us."

Marco offered a case in point.

"During my rookie year I was really struggling. Reggie came up to me at breakfast to encourage me. He told me to just keep doing what I was doing and I would be all right. I guess he saw something in me," Marco reminisced.

"Marco, you wouldn't be here if the Packers thought you couldn't play," Reggie assured him.

As in most other things, White was right.

I asked if he'd ever fallen prey to one of Brett Favre's ruthless pranks.

"Oh man, I heard some real screams coming from over by the stalls. Someone would be just 'taking care of business' and the ice bucket would come down. You'd have thought by all the yelping and bellowing that someone got stabbed or something," he laughed.

Marco Rivera had three straight Pro Bowl seasons from 2002 through

2004. He understood why the Packers let him go, and he trusts the Green Bay fans understood why he couldn't refuse the offer the Dallas Cowboys made him. Injuries halted his career in 2007.

"Let me tell you what, Green Bay is special. Green Bay is #1 in my heart. They have the greatest organization in the world from the top on down. Everything is first class, everything. When you're in Green Bay, you're treated like somebody special, and there are no fans like Packer fans…none!" said a fired-up Rivera.

Today, Marco is surrounded by a wonderful family. He, his wife, Michelle, and their three boys live in Dallas. At this publication, Dante is 10, Roman is 8 and Nico is 5. Marco loves being a husband and dad, and clearly has his priorities in order. He also admits he loves any opportunity to come home and visit with his other family in Green Bay, who own a piece of his heart.

By Steve Rose with memories from Marco Rivera

CR ЯD

63 God, Family and the Green Bay Packers

The hair on the back of my neck loses its curl and I get the traditional chill down my spine every time someone talks about the Green Bay Packer glory years. I was fortunate enough to be growing up during that renowned period of time. The memories can still overwhelm me.

I grew up in Campbellsport, WI, during the 1960s. The Packers were as much a part of everyday life as breathing itself, even during the off season. We looked forward to each week during the fall and early winter months. If we weren't talking about the Packers, we were emulating them in our backyards and on the playgrounds, hanging their posters on our bedroom walls, or collecting their playing cards. We may not have had all the garb and paraphernalia that most kids have today, but that didn't stop our creative juices from flowing.

I remember my neighbor Dean Hadley and I pulled our white socks up over our jeans to make it look like we had on leggings. We were convinced we looked "tough." During halftime of the games, I would con my sister Rita into a game of tackle football in the back yard. Because she was younger and quite a bit smaller than me, I had to play on my knees. I still beat her! (Today she'd probably insist that she "let" me win.)

Vince Lombardi was like a god in our town, and what he said was like gospel to us. When he addressed his players, he often spoke about the three most important things. He adamantly declared, "There are three things that should be important to you in your life. They are your God, your family and the Green Bay Packers, in that order."

Well, the Thelen household had Lombard's three components, but we didn't always have them in the right order. Our order got a little out of whack from time to time. Simply put, most times the Packers were on the top of the list.

Sundays in the fall meant getting up early to attend church. I always liked it when the Packers played at noon. Church began at 11:30 am and usually lasted 45 minutes to an hour, but on Packer Sunday, the priest would shorten or completely eliminate his sermon so we could get home for the kickoff. What a guy! (This is how I have come to believe that God truly is a Packer fan.)

Who could ever forget the music played during the opening kickoff? And Ray Scott's terse, minimalist, but steady voice as he announced, "Starr.........to Dowler........Touchdown!" Hall of Famer Tony Canadeo, who sat alongside Ray for most of the games, was always entertaining and full of Packer knowledge. My heart rate goes up just thinking about the good old days.

Mom and Dad had a black and white Zenith television which seemed as big as our not-so-spacious living room. Dad had three separate remote controls, my sister Renee, my sister Rita and me. I guarantee he had no problem using us and our batteries never wore out.

Most Sunday game days would find us sharing the game with family friends, the Pierrets, Falks, Uelmens and Halfmanns. Metal folding chairs were set up in the living room. It seemed there was enough food to feed 20 families. Brats and hamburgers were on the grill and a keg of Old Timers sat on ice in the wash tub.

We were taught to appreciate the game, and to respect the players and coaches, traits that seem to be in short supply in today's society.

Players seemed more concerned with personal integrity and less concerned about how much money they were making. Everyone seemed to enjoy himself because he was engaged in a game more than a business. I really miss the good old days.

I have always had a strong pride and heartfelt dedication to the Packer organization, so much so that my cousin Mavis and I made a pact together to make at least one away game each year.

We began in Minnesota, and over the years traveled to San Diego, San Francisco, Jacksonville, Chicago, Houston, Miami and many more cities. What initially began as a duo has turned into a full-fledged family event, as several of our cousins began to join us. We had a grand time together.

We've met many Packer greats while travelling with Packer fan tours, including Fuzzy Thurston, Ray Nitschke, Jerry Kramer, Boyd Dowler, Larry McCarren and Wayne Larravie, just to mention a few.

It's been a great experience with absolutely no regrets, and a treasure house full of great green-and-gold memories.

By Rory Thelen

CR SO

**Standing left to right: Rory Thelen, Fuzzy Thurston, Randy Ruplinger, Roger Ruplinger, Tony Ruplinger and Allen Ruplinger.
Kneeling left to right: Matty Thelen and David "Mavis" Ruplinger**

64 A Fun Time With Jerry Kramer

"It's tough putting up with these obnoxious Packer fans!" jokes Jerry Kramer, rather loudly, as he hugs and kisses the top of the head of the diminutive Barbara Mendlesky. Kramer was back in Wisconsin for a 90-minute event in Fond du Lac, signing memorabilia and telling a few stories.

The commentary from the man known for "the block" in the December 31, 1967, Ice Bowl that allowed Bart Starr to score the winning touchdown against the Dallas Cowboys causes the room to erupt with laughter. The 6'3" 74-yr-old made the statement on his way to the door followed by dozens of last-minute well wishes from the fans who are dear to his heart.

Apart from meeting Bart Starr one time briefly at Ray Nitschke's funeral, I've never met any of the other glory day players, those men who played for Vince Lombardi, especially the ones in Super Bowls I & II, both, of course, won by the Packers. In May of 2010 I had the pleasure to meet Jerry Kramer with the help of my brother Gary and Johnny Carey. Gary made the introductions.

"Jerry, Steve Rose. By the way, Carla from the Cheddarhead Pack of Houston says 'hello.'"

"Well, be sure to say hello to Carla for me," he said quite sincerely and graciously.

"Nice to meet you, Steve."

I sat down next to Jerry while he signed various items for Packer fans. Jerry was in his element, enjoying every minute and every fan.

"Claude Crabbe called me the other day and asked me what I was up to. I told him I was going to Green Bay and he says, 'Geez, you haven't played in 50 years.'"

It's safe to say Claude has never been in Green Bay to see how the fans treat their players, both past and current, with incredible appreciation, enthusiasm, respect and dignity.

I asked Jerry what it was like to play for Vince Lombardi.

"Vince could be quite an antagonist. He was always yelling or barking at somebody. It was really stressful playing for him. We didn't learn until later that there was a method to his madness. He knew what he was doing with each of us."

"What was it like playing against some of the all-time greats, like the late Merlin Olson?" I continued to probe.

"We were great competitors on the field, but off the field we were good friends. You get to know and respect each other. For instance, after a game, we'd ask each other about injuries. Once, I admitted that I had some pretty sore ribs and he'd say, 'Yeah, Jerry, I could tell.' Merlin was a very, very nice guy."

Just then, Jerry was approached by a sweet Packer couple in their '70s. "We think the world of Bart Starr."

"I think the world of Bart Starr, too," he said quickly with a broad smile that covered his entire face. "He is one class act."

Jerry leaned over to me and shared the following story.

"Bart was such a field general, a take-charge kinda guy. Honestly, for his first couple of years in Green Bay, he was really kind of quiet and never really got angry. Actually, I joked with others that he was kind of like water, odorless, colorless and tasteless."

Jerry burst into a huge grin.

"I only heard Bart swear one time. We were playing the Chicago Bears at Soldier Field," says Kramer, chewing on a piece of cheese and cracker. "Linebacker Bill George hit Bart after he released the ball. I mean it was definitely a late hit, but in those days they didn't call them. Bart's top lip was split wide open all the way to his nose. George yells to Bart, 'That outta take care of you, you *&%$*.'"

It was then that Jerry heard Bart yell his "choice words" to George. He'd never heard anything like that come out of Bart's mouth either before that or after that.

According to Kramer, Starr was bleeding profusely, so in an effort to be helpful, or at least point out the obvious he offered a suggestion to #15.

"Bart, you better go to the sidelines and get sewn up."

"Well, Bart looked at me and said, 'Just shut up and get in the huddle.' I did, and so did he, with his jersey totally covered in blood."

There's probably more to that story, but I never heard it. Jerry was back to chatting with fans who had come to the table for his autograph.

It's safe to say there will only ever be one Vince Lombardi from the glory day coach era. Unfortunately, Green Bay was not successful under Bart Starr or Forrest Gregg. Kramer feels he has Lombardi to thank for helping to steer him back on track and motivate him in a rather unusual way.

"One day in practice, in '63 or '64, I was having a really bad day. Coach comes running up to me after a play, gets in my face and says, 'A college kid has the attention span of 5-minutes, a high-schooler 3 and a kindergartner 30 seconds...and you, you don't have any!'"

"I lumbered off to the locker room afterward and pretty much came to the conclusion that maybe my career was over. I looked down at my shoes to see if they were shined enough for a job interview. The locker room had cleared out and I'm still sitting there with my hand holding up my chin when Coach comes up to me, and puts his hand on my shoulder," Kramer continued with that reminiscent look on his face.

"Kid, I've seen the best, and you can be one of the best offensive linemen in the National Football League." Lombardi said in a steady and authoritative voice.

"In that moment, I felt a fire and confidence begin to burn in me and from that day on I began to become the player I was meant to be, thanks to Coach Lombardi, the ultimate motivator."

Kramer got to his feet to leave. As he was walking toward the door, it became apparent that he walked with a bit of a limp, a sure sign of the wear and tear the 74-yr-old's body endured from his days on the field.

I doubt, however, if you'll ever hear him complain about his aches and pains. Jerry Kramer lived his dreams on the field, and is still living them today off the field.

If you're not from Wisconsin, where Packers current or former are adored, then you may be in the same boat as Claude Crabbe.

Steve Rose with Jerry Kramer

You may never understand it. You may never get it. But Jerry Kramer sure does.

By Steve Rose

ભ ૪

65 The 65 Roses Green Bay Chapter

Former Packer linebacker John Dorsey was a mean football player. Tim Lewis, who patrolled the defensive backfield, wasn't the nicest man on the field himself. Off the field, however, these fellows were mush, simply mush.

Perry Kidder shared with me the incredible story of how the Green Bay chapter of "65 Roses" got started in the mid '80s with the help of these two top-notch gents. This organization is dedicated to the fight against Cystic Fibrosis, a debilitating disease that is the number-one genetic killer of kids.

You would be right if you are assuming that the Green Bay organization and the players were involved in the process. I listened intently to Perry's exciting rendition of the sequence of events that led to the start of a Green Bay chapter of CF. The national CF had requested that Green Bay join them, but Perry and his pals had another idea.

"A gentleman by the name of Jack Broren, an A-1 first class fellow, was dedicated to the cause of fighting this god-awful disease. He gave me a call and asked me if I would help start a CF chapter in Green Bay. I asked how this would involve me, and he explained that he needed the kind of help I could offer. I was a veteran Green Bay TV boss who'd been in the market for about seven years at the time."

Perry took just enough time to catch his breath and then continued.

"Jack was the president and I was the VP of the local chapter that we were starting. We got some real momentum with the help of Chuck Lane and Tom Olejniczak of the Packers. The board was made of concerned citizens in the Fox River Valley. They were incredibly generous-hearted people."

"The first thing we needed to do was to create an event that would raise money. When the team and the players learned that there were never adults affected by CF (because kids never survived the disease) they got involved, in a big way."

"We called both John Dorsey and Tim Lewis, two of the nicest guys in the world. More than give their time, they gave their hearts, and this wasn't easy work. They really set the tone for this."

Perry contemplatively paused before continuing.

"Many of these kids were knocking on death's door. John and Tim jumped in with both heart and soul." 'Just tell us what we need to do,' they'd say, 'and it's done.'"

"Another thing that was extraordinary was the way the organization was run. Other than the expenses against the golf tournament, there were no expenses against the dollars raised. When we had postage costs, a company would pick that up. If we needed printing, someone would pick up those costs…and so on. It was awesome, and we were proud of that," beamed Kidder.

Now, years later, the cause is still being supported like never before. The head coach of the Packers knows that when he comes to Green Bay, he has his own golf tournament to benefit CF. The last detail is one that Perry seemed most proud of.

"CF board member and physician Dr. Stu Adair from St. Vincent's was the 'go to' man on CF. He kept us up-to-date on the progress in the field. Today there's a CF wing at St. Vincent Hospital in Green Bay, which is a huge benefit to so many because it can be a hardship for some to get to Milwaukee. This wing provides CF patients and their families with the most recent technologies and treatments possible."

Perry continues.

"We also provide funds for our local St. Vincent's medical professionals that treat our CF local patients that give them the opportunity to attend international CF research symposiums. This provides the medical team with the most recent research and treatment for this dreaded disease."

Here is another thought from Kidder.

"The other way that we invest our monies is for CF research. We are fortunate to keep dollars in the state of Wisconsin because the University of WI Madison is one of the foremost research facilities in the world."

So, it's hats off to the Green Bay Packers and hats off, as well, to Perry and his pals, who have kept up the good fight.

There is one other endearing note to the story.

Have you wondered why it's called the 65 Roses Chapter? Some of the younger children could not pronounce the disease, but they could say 65 (Cystic Fi-) Roses (brosis). Ah, from the mouths of babes.

Perhaps the next time you stop by for a tour of Lambeau Field and the Hall of Fame, you also might want to consider a tour of St Vincent's wing affectionately known by its young patients as 65 Roses.

By Steve Rose with memories from Perry Kidder

CR SO

66 Dan's Gifts to Dad & Daughter

August 7, 1992, will always be a special day for me, not only because I interviewed a couple of Packer players and a new coach, but even more so because of what transpired later that day.

At that time, I was the sports editor of the Marshfield News-Herald. The summer slow down for prep events was coming to an end. This, I thought, would be a good time to check out Packer camp. Green Bay opened the 1992 pre-season on Aug. 8 against the Kansas City Chiefs, a perfect opportunity to write a couple of feature stories, as well as an overall story on the beginning of the pre-season.

Mike Holmgren was about to embark on his storied career, although, at the time, none of us were quite sure how good he was going to be. The night before, I drove to Fond du Lac and picked up my dad, Nick, who was 71.

"Dad, how'd you like to join me on a trip to Green Bay?"

"Sure," he said, happily jumping at the opportunity.

We left the following morning. An hour-and-one-half later, we arrived at Lambeau Field. I stopped by the office to pick up my press credential and then Dad and I walked toward the field entrance. The Packers were having a final walk-through at practice that day. Once we got to the gate, I told Dad he'd have to wait for me there, that I'd only be a few moments.

I walked through the stadium and down to the field. I found myself in the end zone, waiting for the players to come by. Chuck Cecil, and a second-year unknown quarterback named Brett Favre, were gracious enough to let me ask each of them a few questions. Cecil, at the time, was a hard-nosed defensive player who clearly wasn't enjoying the Holmgren era yet, and was a bit critical of the new coach.

Next up was Favre.

"All I want is a chance. I've been working hard for Coach Holmgren on the new offense," he calmly told me.

As Brett was talking, a somehow familiar movement caused me to glance to my right. Lo and behold, Dad had wandered on to the field and was standing within feet of me. He wasn't supposed to be there, so I wondered if perhaps he had had a 'senior moment' or something.

The thought, "Oh no, Dad's going to get tossed! This could get ugly real quick!" kept swirling around in my head.

A security guard walked by us and checked to be sure I had my media credentials. Thank goodness, for whatever reason, he never bothered my dad. In fact, Dad ended up watching all three of my interviews, the third being with the first-year coach, Mike Holmgren.

"Dan, who's this with you?" Holmgren asked politely.

"Coach, this is my father, Nick Kohn," I said proudly.

"It's so nice to meet you, Nick." He grinned and the two shook hands.

Instead of getting thrown out, or disciplined, Dad had the time of his life. He was especially impressed with how nice the field was.

"It's like a carpet," he marveled.

Dad had been a season ticket holder in Milwaukee for more than 50 years. Now, for the first time, he had the opportunity to meet a couple of Packer players and a head coach right there on the field.

It's a moment we still talk about.

In September 1996, I'd read in the sports section that Ray Nitschke was scheduled to sign autographs at a store in Wausau. I had met Ray when I had worked for the Fond du Lac Reporter a few years earlier. He was gruff, but begrudgingly allowed for interviews. It was obvious, however, he'd rather have a bad case of indigestion than talk to a young reporter, but he did it just the same.

Ray's always been a favorite of mine, although I was too young to remember the Super Bowl victories from the '60s. My best memory of him was a jarring hit on a Chicago Bear running back in either 1969 or 1970, which caused a fumble.

On this particular day, my plan was to have him sign a couple of autographs and then high-tail it back home. When we arrived in Wausau, however, it became apparent that wasn't going to happen. In fact, it was hard to miss the enormous line that was already forming.

"Are you sure you really want an autograph that badly?" my wife quizzed me.

"We're here now, so we may as well wait," I replied, resigned to my fate.

So we waited, and waited, and waited some more.

Finally, after two and one-half hours, we reached the former Glory Day Packer hero. I reached over the table to give him one of my photos to be signed. In typical Ray Nitschke fashion, he grumbled at me.

"You want your autograph personalized?"

"No. Thanks, anyway," I mumbled, feeling like a six-year-old.

He looked over his glasses at me, signed it, shook my hand and grumbled something else. I don't recall what he said. Or maybe it was just his typical growl.

Sara was next, and got essentially the same treatment, minus the growl.

Last up was my daughter, Rachel.

"Would you like an autograph?" Nitschke inquired of her.

"No," replied Rachel rather timidly.

Ray was clearly puzzled.

"Then, what would you like?" he asked her softly, losing his gruff tone for a moment.

"Can I have your pen?" she asked politely.

Suddenly, Ray's tough-guy approach went right out the window.

"Sure, honey. Here you go," he grinned.

He shook her hand and acted like a perfect gentleman. He talked with us for a quite a few minutes to the chagrin, I'm sure, of the many people still waiting in line behind us.

Rachel asked him several questions, and he answered every one of them, smiling broader and broader after each one.

I asked Ray if he thought the Packers had a chance to ever win another Super Bowl. They had just lost at Minnesota, but he assured me that he believed the 1996 team was good enough to do it. He was right.

Looking back on both of these family stories, I'm so grateful that, while growing up, I was able to accumulate a treasure trove of memories as I watched the Packers on the field. I am, however, even more grateful for the memories and stories that took place off the field.

By Dan Kohn

CR SO

67 Karl Dropped By

I've been privileged and honored to be involved in the Packers organization, so there are a lot of great memories and stories, but one story in particular stands out.

I was a broadcast journalist at WBAY-TV in Green Bay in the early 1980s. As an on-air personality, I was involved in quite a few charity events. That's how I got to know a number of Packers players, their wives and girlfriends. Karl Swanke (Offensive Tackle) and his wife, Maggie, became good friends, and continue to be to this day.

During this time my dad, who lived in suburban Milwaukee, was going through cancer treatment and was having a rough time. The highlight of many of his weeks was watching the Packers on TV.

One weekend, when the Packers were playing a game in Milwaukee, Karl and a few of his Packer friends stopped in to pay a visit to my dad. I knew they might do so, but it wasn't a "for sure" thing, so I hadn't mentioned anything about it to my parents. The looks on both of my parents' faces when Karl and the others walked in the door was priceless!

The fellows sat down and chatted. My dad was literally speechless. When my dad began tiring, they shook his hand, thanked him for being a fan, reminded him to watch the game and left.

For years after that, my dad would proudly tell anyone who would listen about his visit from the Packers.

My mom, also an avid fan, kept telling everyone, "You can't believe how big and tall they were. When they sat down, their heads touched the top of the picture over the couch!"

I especially like this story because it's about a small, but very impactful act of kindness. It's the kind of thing I see many of the players do today, quietly and without fanfare or media attention.

But it's this kind of thing that sets the Packers apart, and why we, their fans, are devoted to them.

By Susan Finco, President, Leonard & Finco Public Relations, Inc.,
Green Bay Packers Board of Directors

CR ЄO

68 Honey, I Kicked in the TV Again!

When you live in Wisconsin, you're automatically a Packer fan. It's a given. I grew up in Iowa, and quickly discovered this "truth" when I moved to Wisconsin in the fall of 1986. Now, I already knew of at least one big Packer fan, Steve Rose. You may recognize his name from the cover of this book! We worked together in the early '80s in Clarion, Iowa, when we were both young radio know-it-alls.

A native of Wisconsin, Steve would regale us with stories of the great Packer tradition. And we'd see his love and fire for them a few Sundays in the fall as he, Steve Autey, Dennis Lowe and I would gather for the Packer games at one of our apartments. Steve would point out coach Bart Starr, tell us what a great guy he was and how he won the Ice Bowl, incessantly, I might add. It might be good to point out at this juncture of the story that we were a very eclectic group as far as allegiances were concerned.

I was a Bengals fan; Autey was from Minneapolis and loved his Vikings (the guy is really in need of help); and Dennis had a Cowboys jersey (poor deceived fellow). I never would have imagined I would someday live in Wisconsin, but as alluded to in the beginning, I got my chance in the 'mid to late '80s. I would witness, first hand, "Packermania."

Let me share a couple of stories that I think epitomize the personality of Packer fans. A nice and passionate guy I worked with at KFIZ-AM in Fond du Lac, whom I'll call him Jim, grew up in Wisconsin and had gone to UW-Madison. Like most Packer fans and Wisconsonites, Jim was a die-hard Packer fan who had, shall we say, a couple of overly-competitive quirks.

One afternoon, a fellow golf partner, Greg, and I saw Jim throw hundreds of dollars worth of gear in the water on the golf course! Based on this display of temper, you may find it no big surprise then that on occasion Jim caused some damage to more than one television set during the Packer seasons. You're welcome to use your imagination as to how they would meet their final demise, but I can tell you it involved a boot to the tube and a mid-air flight off the TV stand. I'm pretty sure, knowing Jim, that the GE screen would have "hooked" before hitting the floor!

Another time, a Packer fan was driving a group of us to his place for the game. We got a later-than-anticipated start. Not wanting to miss the kickoff, let's just say he was going a bit beyond the speed limit. His poor wife could be heard yelling from the backseat.

"Slow down! Are you trying to get us all killed?!"

We did make it for the game – and we were on time for the kickoff.

Mind you, I'm not condoning this kind of behavior, but Packer fans in particular may remember that this was the mid '80s (the frustrating "Forrest" years) where the green-and-gold was good at grabbing defeat out of the jaws of victory toward the end of games. Knowing Steve, I suspect there may be a few other stories here in this great collection where an individual or family may have needed an "intervention," or a "Packer Anger Management" session or two.

These days I'm back home in Fort Dodge, IA. I have to confess that, along with my Bengals, I really do love following and even watching the Packers because of my time spent in Wisconsin.

I would like to offer a few tips for anyone who may be planning to visit or possibly even live in Wisconsin. When the golf courses are green, or the green-and-gold is playing, if a guy named Jim asks if you want to play a round of golf…uh…tell you him you have other plans. And, if he invites you over for a Packer game, make sure you have a backup plan - or he has a second TV.

As for me, I'm praying that if I ever go to Jim's place again for a game, he'll at least find it a bit more difficult to reach up to kick that 52-inch flat screen TV, although I'm still fairly certain that his kick will "hook" anyway!

By Bill Grady

CR ƧO

69 Bradd's Dream

When little eight-year-old Bradd Martin from Clarion, IA, visited friends in Neenah, WI, in 1984, little could he have known he would leave town having been bitten by the Packer bug. He's not alone. It happens all the time. After following the green-and-gold for nearly 16 years, it was only a few years ago that the 34-year-old got to live his dream of coming to Green Bay and the hallowed ground of Lambeau Field.

Bradd had no particular allegiance to any NFL team while growing up in the cornfields of north central Iowa. The games on TV on Sundays were usually of the Vikings, Bears, Chiefs and the occasional Packer game. Frankly, until the summer of 1984, he didn't really care. His father, Gary, had raised him to be an Iowa Hawkeyes fan, but both he and his dad were relatively neutral where an NFL team was concerned, until, that is, 1984.

"We were at a practice and I could see James Lofton and Lynn Dickey walking off the field. I was so close to them I could have almost reached out and touched them. They seemed so big. We also went to the Hall of Fame. That was cool, too. I remember kicking some footballs there. And the memorabilia was awesome! That's when it all started. When I got home, I entered the Packer phase of my life," Bradd recalls nearly 26 years later.

There were a few lean years during the Forrest Gregg era, but then things changed, and his Packermania went to a whole new level.

"My friends would tease me quite a bit when the Packers struggled in the mid to late '80s, but when the 1989 season was over, they weren't picking on me anymore. As a matter of fact, a few of them became fans. Don Majkowski had an awesome year, and the team won a series of really close games and nearly made the playoffs. Until then, there were only a handful of Packer fans in our town, but the numbers increased dramatically after that. But I was the first!"

Over the next three years, in the early part of the '90s, things really got exciting for Bradd and the Packer faithful.

"The September 20, 1992, Packer game was on the local TV station. It was Brett's first game. He made a phenomenal pass to Kittrick Taylor and the team won 24-23, and the rest is history. From that time on, I was a huge Favre fan. Well, I suppose that changed a bit in 2009 when he went to the Vikings," he laughs.

Those years in the mid '90s were exhilarating. The Packers won one Super Bowl against the New England Patriots and had another slip away against the Denver Broncos. That little setback, however, did nothing to squelch Bradd's fervor for the Packers, not one iota. In fact, his allegiance and love for the team only deepened and heightened his desire to come to Lambeau Field for a game.

"I nearly made it up for the Minnesota vs. Green Bay game in 2000, when Antonio Freeman made that miraculous catch. I had tickets, but the problem was I couldn't get anyone to make the trip with me. I never gave up my dream that one day I would be able to make it to Green Bay for a game," he recalled.

Over the years, Bradd has always been happy to read about the Packers calling up players from his home state of Iowa. Homegrown Iowa boys include Bryce Paup, Adam Timmerman, Ross Verba and Aaron Kampman. While Bradd appreciates them all, he does have a favorite.

"Aaron Kampman is so down-to-earth and genuine. When we had the floods in '07, he came back home to help. When his coach at Parkersburg, Ed Thomas, got killed, he came back home. We're really proud that he's one of us. I hope he does well in Jacksonville, except against the Packers, of course." (Kampman signed with the Jaguars in Free Agency in March

In January of '08, Bradd finally caught the Packer break he was looking for.

"I was sitting at home, trying to figure out what the end of the '08 season would look like. The playoff picture was pretty jumbled up. Finally, they announced that the Packers were going to be playing the Seattle Seahawks at Lambeau. I figured Brett was close to retiring (guess I called that one wrong) and I knew that if I didn't do this now, I may never do it. So, I asked my friend, Jason, if he wanted to go to Lambeau with me and he said, 'Yeah, sure I'll go.'"

The search for tickets began. Bradd navigated through search engines on the internet to every site he could find. Finally he hit the jackpot.

"I found seats that were four rows up in the end zone, the one right down near the Packer tunnel. We came up the night before and stayed in Neenah, a half hour south of Green Bay. We picked up our tickets the next day, and confirmed that they were legit. Jason and I were starting to get pumped," remembers Martin.

Their seats were everything they could have hoped for.

"It was unbelievable. I got some great pictures of Kampman and Favre coming out of the tunnel. Then I saw Kampman doing some wind sprints not far from me."

It was then that Martin had a tiny slip of the tongue.

"Being from Iowa and a Hawkeye fan when Aaron played there, I thought I'd get his attention by yelling 'Go Hawks!' He looked at me a bit strangely as did a few people around me. Then it hit me. The Packers were playing the Seahawks! Whoops! It was a total 'duh' moment," Bradd laughed.

As it began to snow, Bradd called his dad to tell him he felt like he was on the best part of the planet at the moment.

"Dad, it's beginning to snow here. I can't believe it. Here I am, at Lambeau Field, watching a Packer game. It doesn't get any better than this. I couldn't ask for anything better. The atmosphere is positively electric. I have goose bumps, and it's not from the cold," he told Gary, who was watching the game from back home in Iowa.

Any true Packer fan will recall that the beginning of the game was a disaster, an absolute nightmare, as the Seahawks capitalized on turnovers and took a quick 14-0 lead, but neither Bradd nor the faithful lost heart. The Packers had a 28-17 lead at halftime, and the Packers continued to pour it on, winning 42-20. Bradd watched as the snow fell so heavily at times he could barely see the players. It didn't matter. He was at Lambeau, and that's what truly mattered.

As Bradd reflects on that wonderful time, he admits that he never would have imagined that trip to Wisconsin to visit friends in '84 would become the catalyst to convert him to a die-hard Packer fan, but that's exactly what happened.

"I love the Packers. I always will and I hope to get back to Green Bay someday for another game. But, if I don't, I will still have those memories, snowy ones at that. How many people are fortunate enough to love this team from afar and then have the opportunity to watch a game of the magnitude that Jason and I did? It was a dream come true, man, a dream come true."

By Steve Rose with memories from Bradd Martin

CR ЕО

Bradd Martin standing outside of Lambeau Field

70 Andy & Reggie in the Same Room

The year was 1997, and I was 10 years old. My father was director of network development for Winners Success Radio Network. He also engineered WSN's Leap of Faith Sports Radio Show, at the time in its second season. Several years have passed, so most memories of that day have vanished from my memory. However, because of a very special photograph and a one-of-a kind pigskin, I won't ever completely forget what happened on that late '90s fall Monday.

I was encouraged to record some of my experiences from that day for this book, but I didn't think I would discover anything significant until I listened to a tape of what was recorded on that out-of-the-ordinary Monday. One of the guests on the show was none other than Packer Defensive End Reggie White, or "The Minister of Defense" as he was affectionately known in Packerland. I was at the studio the day of the taping to soak in the experience, meet Reggie, and get his autograph.

Listening to the tape reminded me of just how special this man really was. He wasn't afraid to share his faith in Christ. More than that, Reggie's definition of faith was not what you might expect. During the program, he recounted that those listed as faithful saints in the Bible were

Bob Gardinier, Andy Gardinier and Reggie White

credited with faith not because they believed God was going to do something for them, but because they did what God told them to do.

We hear a lot about how the Green Bay Packers have the greatest fans in professional football. In my opinion, that's tough to measure. No doubt Packers fans are spectacular. But I suggest that Green Bay has been blessed to have had some of the greatest individuals to have ever played the game grace the grassy stage at 1265 Lombardi Avenue. They're known not only for their phenomenal NFL skills, but for their amazing character. Reggie White certainly fit that description. He let some of that character shine on that particular Monday in the studio, and I have a signed football to remind me.

By Andy Gardinier

CR BO

71 Fryman Family Fun

It was the 1996 opening day for the Milwaukee Brewers baseball team at County Stadium. My father-in-law had invited me to the game. Standing on the mound, ready to throw out the first pitches were Packer players LeRoy Butler and Robert Brooks. For those of you who may not make the correlation, they are the two credited with starting the Lambeau Leap. LeRoy made the leap once in '93. Robert liked it, perfected it, and you know the rest of the story.

Both Packers had been invited to throw out the first pitches because the team had had a wonderful season the year before. I suspect it's rare that any other NFL players have done this in other major league parks, but as you have come to know by now, the Green Bay Packers have quite an effect in Wisconsin, the USA and throughout the world.

Post game we went to a bar for a sandwich and libation.

"Who is that over there?" I questioned my father-in-law.

"I'm not sure," he replied.

Then it dawned on me.

"That's Robert Brooks and Craig Newsome!" I blurted out excitedly.

I grabbed my stepson, Joe, who was wearing a Packer jacket.

"Hey, let's go get some autographs," I suggested as we approached Brooks.

"Mr. Brooks, could you autograph Joe's jacket. please?"

"That'll cost you a round of drinks for everyone at the table," he smiled. "No, the kids are free," he joked, an award-winning grin covering his face.

Mind you, I would have happily obliged Brooks' request. I would have thought it was the least I could do. I don't think any of us have a clue what it must be like to be approached as often Packer players are. I can tell you this, however. Every time I've approached a player, he's always been very polite and gracious. I know, from experience, that this is not always the case in other towns or with other teams.

Brooks shook my hand and then pulled out a black marker that looked like it was two feet long! He grabbed Joe by the shoulders, picked him up off the ground, and held him in the air while Craig Newsome signed first. Then Craig held Joe while Brooks signed. I'll never forget Joe's jacket getting signed while he was still in it, his little legs dangling in the air! It's a day neither of us will ever forget.

The following year I took my family to Packer camp to watch the players' bike from the Lambeau facility to the training field. While there we spotted Coach Mike Holmgren who came over to the fence and chatted with us for about 15 minutes. I couldn't help but notice there was a young man standing all alone in back of us wearing a #8 Green Bay Packer jersey. I turned around to him and extended my hand to him.

"What's your name?" I asked.

"Uh…my name is Ryan Longwell. I'm here to see if I can be the kicker for the Packers."

"It's nice to meet you, Ryan," I said. "Good luck. Give it your best."

Who would have thought that this seemingly shy, unimposing young man would spend the next nine years as a successful kicker for the Green Bay Packers? And I got to shake his hand when no one seemed to care who he was.

My advice is to pay close attention to the "kid" in the Packer jersey standing next to you. You never know. He could be one of the next green-and-gold stars!

By Keith Fryman

CR EO

72 Robert Leaps to Green Bay

Robert Brooks played a key role in the resurgence of the Packers' popularity in the 1990s. After Sterling Sharpe was forced to retire, following the 1994 season due to a neck injury, Robert stepped into a starting wide receiver position. He had a breakthrough year in 1995 with 102 receptions for nearly 1,500 yards. Following that season, Robert signed on as a spokesperson for Alphorn Ford in Monroe and Rapids Ford in Wisconsin Rapids, both under the same ownership.

Working as a broadcaster at WEKZ in Monroe, I had the pleasure of meeting Robert when he made a personal appearance at Alphorn Ford in May 1996. He regaled us with accounts of the games from the previous season, and with commentary about his relationship with God. His enthusiasm for both was contagious.

Both Robert and the Packers were having another great season in 1996 when, in the seventh game, he suffered a torn ACL and patella tendon while blocking 49er Tyronne Drakeford on a running play. Unfortunately, Robert missed the rest of that season, but the Packers went on to win the Super Bowl. Despite the injury, Robert came to Monroe again that fall for another personal appearance at Alphorn Ford. He talked passionately about his faith in God and how God would help him recover from his injury. Those of us who spoke with him were completely convinced Robert would come back better than ever.

The 1997 season began with a Monday night game at Lambeau Field against the Chicago Bears. WEKZ put together an overnight bus trip for area fans to attend the game. We had a lot of Robert Brooks fans on that trip, hoping to see Robert do well in his first game back since he had suffered the injury. With the score tied 11-11 in the second quarter (that's right...it was the only time in NFL history that any game had that specific score) Robert hauled in an 18-yard touchdown pass from Brett Favre to give the Packers the lead.

After catching that pass, Robert pointed to his knee and then pointed to the sky, a clear indication that he was thanking God for healing his knee. The Packers won that game 38-24. Robert Brooks was back and so were the Packers. They went 13-3 and were again on their way to another Super Bowl appearance. Robert also won the NFL Comeback Player of the Year award for the 60 passes he caught for over 1,000 yards.

Another highlight of that season was a 45-17 win over the Dallas Cowboys. It was the Cowboys' first game at Lambeau Field since the Ice Bowl. The Packers had lost eight straight games to the Cowboys before the November 23rd game. One thing I remember about that game was that Steve Rose had a speaking engagement in the Monroe area that weekend, so he came to my apartment afterward to watch that game where Robert had one reception for 36 yards.

But the best part about that game was the fact that the Cowboy monkey was off the back of the team and Steve and I got to watch that game together, even if it was some three hours south of the shadows of Lambeau Field.

By Mark Evenstad

CR SO

73 The Sunday School Lesson

Ten-year-old Tim Trauger noticed something quite peculiar as his family headed north on US Highway 41 between Oshkosh and Green Bay.

"Mom, there aren't any cars going the same way we are," he observed, although there was bumper to bumper traffic going south.

"Honey, now that you mention it, there aren't," she agreed.

Did we mention that it was about 3 in the afternoon on Sunday, October 15, 1967? As any true Packer fan knows, what this was really about is the fact that nearly half of everyone in the area was at Lambeau Field for the Packer-Viking game.

Tim shared this story with me over a bowl of his delicious made-from-scratch soup. His mother, Jeane Trauger, was transporting her family of four kids from the greater Cincinnati area of Ohio, where they had been residing, in order to live where Jeane considered "back home." On board with the recent widow were her children Melissa, Steve, Tim and David. Jeane was taking her family back to New London, WI, the place where she had grown up. Her husband, Calvin, had passed away a year earlier.

I've known Tim and Kathy Trauger for almost five years now. I'm a regular at their establishment, CSI, an Appleton café whose name stands for Cookies-Soup-Ice Cream. Their soup is second to none. I encouraged Tim to develop a Packer Pea Soup recipe that we could share with our readers, and he did. You'll find it following this story.

"Did I ever tell you the Sunday School story?" Tim asked me.

"I don't think so," I replied, sipping on some Shrimp Florentine.

"I attended Sunday School at the Congregational United Church of Christ. One Sunday, Mr. Cy Kluever had a question for our group."

"Can anyone give me the name of a great NFL quarterback?"

"Johnny Unitas!" I yelled without a moment's hesitation.

Wrong answer!

Did we mention that Tim was a Baltimore Colts fan?

The steely gazes he got and the stern explanation as to why his answer was wrong scared him right into reality! The temperature in the room dropped so dramatically that it was a preview of the Ice Bowl to come two months later. He had unabashedly declared that there was another quarterback other than the great Bart Starr! Suddenly Tim realized he wasn't in Ohio anymore!

It didn't take the Traugers long to realize that the Green Bay Packers were second only to God around here, and that the tradition of the green-and-gold went really deep.

"I can be a little slow sometimes, but trust me. I got it!" Tim laughed.

Today, Tim and his wife, Kathy, are full-fledged Packer fans, but Tim will never forget the day he gave the "wrong answer" in Sunday school.

By Steve Rose with memories from Tim Trauger

Tim's Packer Pea Soup Recipe

This is a soup that people always request at Tim's Packer parties, his famous Green and Gold Split Pea Soup.

To feed a dozen people you will need about two gallons of soup, perhaps less if your friends bring food, too.

This recipe can be done in your Nesco.

4 pounds split green peas

2 large onions, chopped not minced

3 large carrots, again chopped, 1/2" to 1"

Most of one bunch of celery. Take a couple stalks for your
veggie tray, chop the rest. Use the light green leaves, too. The
dark ones will be bitter.

Olive oil and a couple pounds of a decent smoked ham.

Slice ham 1/2 inch thick, then cube it.

Sautee veggies in the olive oil til they get soft. This will take about 30-45 minutes and you'll have to stir it a few times.

When the veggies are soft, getting just a little golden brown around the edges, add the peas, ham, and enough water to cover everything, plus an inch or so. You can add more later, but it takes a long, long time to cook it out.

In a couple of hours, it should be done. Add some salt and black pepper to taste. If the water did get away on you, throw in a little bit of Instant Mashed Potatoes. If you find you did not add enough water, simply add a bit more.

A hint. There are a variety of soup bases available, but I like one called Better than Boullion. This is how you should pick your soup base. Don't choose anything called a cube, or that comes in powdered form. They are all salt. Instead, read the labels and find a brand that has (in this case) ham, as its first ingredient. It will be a wet to solid paste. Use a tablespoon at a time until you get the flavor you're looking. All kinds of flavors can be found. Beef, chicken, lobster, etc.

CR SO

74 Wise in His Goings

I was talking with a gentleman recently who admitted his regret for telling off his boss on the way out the door of the company for which he'd been working. I believe the common expression for that activity is called "burning bridges." Not a wise thing to do if avoidable.

The inevitability of professional football and its employees is they may come to the end of their time in a certain city with a certain team, sometimes by design, sometimes not. It's happened a few times in Green Bay. In March of 2010, Aaron Kampman made what many considered, even die-hard Packer fans, a wise business decision when he departed the shadow of Lambeau for Jacksonville, FL.

In working with Packer players over the years, I could easily make a case that the players who originate from Iowa seem to be some of the most grounded that I've met. I never had the privilege of meeting Aaron (though I always wanted to) so I can say that initially I felt some genuine regret when I first heard of his departure from the team, but all of that vanished when I opened the March 20th Milwaukee Journal and read the following letter to Packer fans and the people of Wisconsin.

"I wanted to take a moment to thank you for your support, encouragement and friendship. It's been an honor to serve this community for the past eight years as a member of the legendary Green Bay Packers organization. Linde and I thank God for the years we spent in Wisconsin and we thank you for welcoming us to Wisconsin with open arms.

For my family, this has been so much more than a job. We experienced many public and private successes that will stand in our memories forever. Most importantly, we experienced them with you.

I look forward to the day when I'll bring my three boys to Lambeau Field and reminisce about what it was like to be part of the great Packer Nation."

There is a scripture that speaks to the importance of being wise in our comings and goings. Clearly, Aaron displayed such wisdom when his time in Green Bay ended. In the past, former players who wore the green-and-gold have been invited back. If this should happen for Aaron Kampman, I have no doubt there would be a welcome mat put out, and, as the saying goes, "we'll leave the light on."

I know Packer fans nationwide join me in wishing Aaron, Linde and his three boys every success in all they undertake and everywhere they go. What a class act he is. It's unfortunate that there are fewer and fewer athletes in professional sports who exhibit such wisdom, class and character as did Aaron Kampman. He will be missed.

By Steve Rose

CR Ю

75 The Smell of Packer Incense

During the 1960s, the Green Bay Packers were riding high, and Coach Vince Lombardi was catapulted into virtual sainthood. On the field, he was a gruff taskmaster, to be sure. That was his style. As the wins mounted, so did everyone's appreciation of him. Off the field, he was regarded as a family man who had once studied for the priesthood. He was considered by most to be a person of strong Christian principles.

My father, also a devout Catholic, held Lombardi in high esteem both as a coach and as a man. It was general knowledge that the late coaching great attended daily Mass at St. Willebrord Catholic Church in Green Bay. Lombardi's name came up during sermons in churches throughout the Green Bay Diocese as someone to emulate, not only as a winner, but as a role model to fathers, as well.

During Lombardi's years with the Packers (1959-67), my father managed to acquire a couple of season tickets located on the 40-yard line. However, the players appeared awfully small because our seats were in Row 59 of the 60-row stadium.

Television didn't rule the National Football League as much as it does today, and the review of plays was a rarity. Kickoffs at Lambeau Field were at 1:06 p.m. Because my father was a faithful member of the adult choir at St. John's Church in Little Chute, WI, we always attended 10:30 a.m. Mass followed by benediction. So, before we left for church, my mother would pack a lunch for those of us attending the game.

After the regular Mass was completed, benediction consisted, in part, of the priest slowly swinging a monstrance that emitted the strong smell of burning incense. Services at the Little Chute church often didn't end until 11:45 a.m., which meant we had to really hustle in order to cover the 30-mile trip and arrive by kickoff time.

By the time we did arrive, tailgating had already ended and the stadium was nearly filled. On the way up to our lofty seats, the game-day smells became quite evident. The aroma of burgers, hotdogs and charcoal wafted through the air. Smoking was permitted in those days, so you could easily pick up the smell of cigarettes and strong cigars. Many fans enjoyed drinking beer, while others packed flasks of alcohol to protect them from the cold, making it easy to pick up the smell of alcohol, too.

But with all of these earthly smells quite evident, we brought a bit of Lombardi's Catholic upbringing with us. We had the sweet smell of incense all over us!

By Dan Vander Pas, Appleton Post Crescent

CR SO

76 Bob's Keys of Kindness

In the early '80s, Dan Derks worked for Moe Northern Company in Appleton, purchased by Bob Skoronski, #76 left tackle of the glory day Packers.   Dan remembers those early morning sales meetings.

"You didn't want to be late on Bob's watch, but if you worked hard you were rewarded greatly," recalls Dan. "If you were ever in need, you could count on Bob to help."

Dan's young son, Joey, found it a bit difficult to believe that his dad was working for a Packer, much less one of such renown. He was so skeptical that he had a plan to flush out the facts. Joey's sister, Julie, found a letter Joey had drafted to send to Bob. Keep in mind this is from a six-year-old boy, written in about 1992.

Dear Bob,

Please singure this picture I bought at the mall at a Green Bay Packer story too bad you don't play for the Packers I bet you would be rille happy to win a sopur bowl. And I'm going to win a sopur bowl. And I'm Dan Derk's kid he says you are a very good Boss to bad I didn't work for you I wish I could meet you these day when I'm very old. My dad says you would sing this for me it would mean a lot to me my dad old bosses singure and there is some boxes at moses (Moe Northern) for you. Come and get them one day and mabe I would see you if you can come and get the boxes.

Your friend,

Joey Derks

Interesting what runs through a six-year-old mind, isn't it?

For Dan, winter mornings in Wisconsin would slap him in the face early, sometimes as early as 5a.m. After working his way from loading dock to an inside sales position, Dan was offered an opportunity to be in outside sales.

"Think you could do my sales route, Dan?" Bob asked.

"Sure, I'd love the chance," Dan replied to the man for whom he had such great respect.

On a cold 20-degree-below-zero morning, Dan set out in his 1983

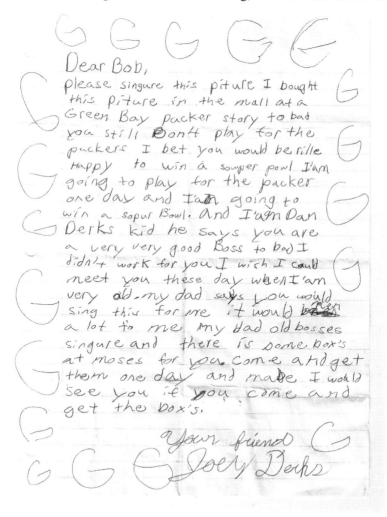

Joe Derks' letter to Bob Skoronski

Dodge Aries for Sheboygan, 90 minutes to the east. Dan was expected to be back by noon to relieve the counter person for lunch, but his car didn't have the mustard to handle the freezing conditions. As a matter of fact, the car stalled and nearly died on the way there. Fortunately, he was only a short distance from Bob's residence and was able to make it that far. Bob's wife, Ruth Ann, answered the door.

"Bob's downstairs on the treadmill," she told him.

Dan headed down the steps to tell his boss of his dilemma. As he talked, Bob never lost a beat on the exercise machine.

"Dan, go, find my coat. There are some keys in the pocket. There's a new Chevy wagon in the garage. Take it, it's yours."

Dan was speechless. His car was towed to the junk yard, and he was back on the road in his new wheels, headed to Sheboygan.

"Bob was great with his employees. I loved listening to his Packer stories over lunch at VanAbels Supper Club," he said gratefully. "But, the best story I can offer is the one about the day he gave us that gift. We'll never forget that."

As for Joey's letter, he never did get a response from Bob, for good reason. He never sent it. I guess he decided to trust that his father really did work for one of the kindest, most generous men to play for the Green Bay Packers.

By Steve Rose with memories from Dan Derks
& Julie (Derks) Stoegerer

CR ED

77 Reminiscing with Dr. Michels

It had been a few years since I'd heard the voice of one of the greatest blessings to ever come through Green Bay for me.

"John!" I answered, seeing his name on my phone's caller ID.

"Steve!" he shot back.

"Buddy, many years ago I wondered what you would be when you grew up," I joked. "So, what are you doing these days?" I quizzed.

"I'm a doctor," he said proudly.

I already knew that, but I wanted to give him a chance to say it so we could both be proud.

Meet John Spiegel Michels, one of the greatest Green Bay Packers of all time. You may be saying to yourself, 'You serious?' Yeah, I am.

This father of three and husband of one, Melissa, is now a doctor of diagnostic radiology at Baylor College of Medicine in Houston, TX. The road to get there has been a struggle, not unlike his NFL career, but John has persevered, and is enjoying his life.

I was introduced to John Michels on October 7, 1996, by a mutual friend and Packer, Ken Ruettgers. Ken was my radio co-host of the TimeOut show on Q-90 from '94-'95. Ken's status as a player was questionable by '96, which put the co-hosting job up for grabs, so John stepped in and took the reins while Ken took some time off in order to sort a few things out. (Ken eventually retired as a Packer in November of '96, leaving John to co-host with me for the duration of the time the show aired.)

Michels was courted by the Packers in the spring of 1996. They flew John into Green Bay a few weeks prior to the draft. One detail he recalls from that visit was that he was given a book, *Home Field Advantage*, written by someone he'd eventually get to know pretty well, Ken Ruettgers. John was taken by the Packers with the 27th pick of the '96 draft out of USC where his stock had risen quickly in his senior year. He remembers draft day as if it was yesterday.

"The commissioner, Paul Tagliabue, had just said Ray Lewis was the 26th pick. We had an inkling we would be next, so we put slices of American cheese on our forehead. Then the phone rang. It was Ron Wolf," remembers John.

Next he heard the words he'll never forget.

"With the 27th pick in the 1996 draft, the Green Bay Packers select John Michels from the University of Southern California," said Commissioner Tagliabue.

The original plan, as John recalls, was that he was to follow in the footsteps of Kenny Ruettgers, the 12-year veteran at left tackle. Ken had considered retirement, but the team convinced Ken to come back for another year to mentor Michels both on and off the field. The on-the-field part fell a bit short when Ken's left knee would not allow him to compete at the level he wanted to, so John was pressed into action. Football issues aside, John and Ken remain best friends to this day.

John started nine games as he helped the Packers win Super Bowl XXXI. He was also the 1996 Co-Rookie of the year and earned NFL All-Rookie honors. In 1997, he returned as the starting left tackle for the first five games of the season before he injured his right knee against the Detroit Lions. He was out for the rest of the season. He was having a great training camp in '98 when he reinjured his knee, forcing him to spend the year on injured reserve.

Even now, John believes that with a healthy knee he would have been able to do quite well in his career with Green Bay, so it was painful to hear the critics say that he was a 'bust.'

"I was an angry, bitter and miserable man. I still held to the belief that God had a bigger plan for my life than just playing a game, but I admit it took me a few years to be able to even watch the Packers play, it really did," John acknowledged.

With his NFL and football career over, John and his wife, Melissa, sat down to discuss what to do with the rest of his life. His decision would not only impact them, but their three children, as well. In 2002, having done youth ministry for two years, they decided that John would return to school to study to become a doctor.

And on a more personal note, I've been waiting many years to tell the Packer nation that one of the most significant blessings to me and my life was John Michels. He did the radio show from '96 to '97, but he also helped to launch something that was a very special experience for me.

In the spring of 1998, I asked the director of Network Development for our radio show, Bob Gardinier, to call all the Green Bay TV stations to setup appointments for me to pitch a Leap of Faith TV show. John had told me he would co-host a TV show with me, if we could get one, so Bob set up interviews at each Green Bay station.

I assumed the process for such an adventure would be lengthy, but barely three minutes into the first meeting with WLUK's GM, Jim Schuessler, he said, "Great, when can we get started start?" I called Bob and asked him to cancel the other appointments. He didn't believe me.

That TV program was as successful as it was because of John. He invited player guests to appear with us every week. Letters came in telling us that lives were being blessed and people were coming to a saving knowledge of Jesus Christ. So, for me, John Michels was one of the finest Green Bay Packers to ever grace the town of Green Bay and the sod of Lambeau Field while he was here.

These days, if you want to see John, you'll have to look him up in the directory at the Baylor College of Medicine. If you do see him, be sure to call him Dr. John, and be sure to tell him there's a farm boy from Wisconsin who is ever grateful for the help he provided to him and for the work he did for the kingdom of God from 1996-1999.

Steve Rose and John Michels

By Steve Rose with memories from John Michels

☙ ❧

78 Tribute to Grandpa

My earliest memories of the Green Bay Packers were of sitting in front of the TV with my grandpa. I grew up in Madison, WI. My grandparents, Alma and Henry Homburg, lived on a farm in Cottage Grove. It was common for my family to spend Sunday afternoons at their farm, where Grandpa and I would cheer and yell together while watching Packers games. Unfortunately, by the time I was old enough to understand and appreciate football, the success of the Lombardi years had passed.

Grandpa and I spent more time yelling at and being frustrated with the Packers than cheering for them. A shared passion for the Packers forged a common connection between us. Grandpa took me to my first Packer game at Milwaukee County Stadium. We joined a bus load of Packer fans from where my grandpa used to work. I could barely contain my excitement. What a great experience it was to see the Packers in person rather than on TV. It wasn't until much later that I learned my ticket almost went to someone else. Grandpa was so worried that he would have to tell me that I couldn't go, knowing how disappointed I would have been.

I had the opportunity to go to the Packer Hall of Fame with my grandparents and uncle. To see the history of the Packers and the great players who are honored there was a special memory for me. I was a young adult when my grandpa and I traveled to the Pro Football Hall of Fame in Canton, Ohio. Naturally, our focus was on the many Packers enshrined there. There were frequent conversations between Grandpa and me critiquing the Packer players and games throughout the years. It was one of the many pleasures of our relationship.

I was back in my grandparents' living room when the Packers lost to Denver in the Super Bowl. As disappointing as the loss was, it was yet another special time shared with my grandpa.

Today, I am fortunate to be a season ticket holder. My only regret is that, because of Grandpa's difficulty walking and other health issues, we weren't able to see a game together at Lambeau Field.

Grandpa Homburg has since passed away, but as I reflect on my many memories of him and our relationship, it becomes apparent how interwoven the Packers are into those memories. Whether the Packers were winning or losing, they represented a shared interest and passion between a grandpa and his grandson.

I know there are many reasons that the Packers are a special team to its fans, and to the state of Wisconsin. There are, undoubtedly, many stories just like mine, which demonstrate how the Packers can bring people together, just like Grandpa and me.

By Steve Lande

CR SO

79 The Four Packateers

Over a span of about 13 years, we (Mike and Nancy Pfeifer, Tim & Cindy McGray and other friends and relatives) have been fortunate to travel to many Packer road games. We didn't always bring a victory back with us, but we certainly brought back our share of lasting memories, and we met some delightful and interesting people along the way. We've traveled to Minneapolis, Cleveland, Miami, Cincinnati, Boston, Tampa (twice), New Orleans, Carolina, Indianapolis, St. Louis, Dallas, San Diego and Arizona. No matter in what city we found ourselves, we discovered a few things to be consistently true. There are a lot of other fans from Wisconsin who make the trips, and there are plenty of Packer fans in other cities all over the USA.

A typical trip's adventures began when we would enter an establishment in the competitor's town. We'd definitely get some looks wearing our green-and-gold. It wouldn't be long, however, before other Packer fans from Wisconsin and die-hards living in that city would be sharing in our excitement. It's been fun, and somewhat fascinating, to watch strangers become friends so quickly.

While in St. Louis, we stayed in a hotel right next to the RCA Dome. It was there that we got to know Connie and Barbie, who were working in the hotel lounge. Of course, they were bragging up their Rams as much as we were our Packers. They mentioned that the Rams' coaching staff always came in for dinner after home games, and that they knew them well. Although we're not gamblers, the night prior to game day, Tim and Mike made a wager with the girls. Should their team lose, the St Louis girls would wear Packer shirts right after the game. Should we lose, Tim and Mike would spend the night in Rams jerseys.

Fortunately for Tim and Mike, the Packers did win the game. Connie and Barbie donned on the green and gold, but they also made it perfectly clear to the customers that they lost a bet. The best part was the Rams coaching staff did come in that same night and had to see the girls in the Packer jerseys. Connie and Barbie were such good sports, as are many of the people we have met around the country.

It's amazing who we meet when we're on the road following our beloved Pack. After attending the Super Bowl in New Orleans in 1997, we four, like many other Packer fans, made our way to visit Brett Favre's home town of Kiln, MS. That meant, of course, a trip to the Broke Spoke, a popular local Packer hangout. Mike paid a visit to the restroom, glanced at the gentleman standing next to him, and realized it was none other than Fuzzy Thurston. It's not every day you get to, well, stand next to a Packer great while taking care of business! Fuzzy later posed for a picture with us.

Mike likes to tell the story of our trip to San Diego for the Super Bowl. We spent a few days seeing the sights of the area, including the famous San Diego zoo. While Cindy and I were walking along taking in the animals and the scenery, we suddenly realized the fellows weren't behind us. What Cindy and I hadn't realized is that we had just walked right past the legendary Bart Starr! The guys, of course, spotted him right away. Bart was incredibly gracious, stopped to talk, and posed for a picture. Unfortunately, Bart's friend took the picture and Cindy was inadvertently cut off, but she relished the opportunity, like the rest of us, to simply meet this Packer great.

One of our favorite friends is "Kelly." Dick Calaway owns Kelly's Bar on Hwy 57, just south of DePere. He's a retired principle from the Wrightstown school district. Kelly's Bar is only open after Packer home

Left to right: Mike and Nancy Pfeifer, Cindy and Tim McGray

games and sometimes on Friday nights after Dick returns from having a fish supper. It's quite an experience stopping at his place. Everything is a dollar; soda, mixed drinks and beer. Kelly's is a well-kept secret. Or, it was until now.

It's been a wonderful ride following our Packers and we hope there are more trips to come.

If you're out and about, and happen to see two guys who look and sound like they might be from Wisconsin, but they're wearing Vikings jerseys, you'd be making a safe bet that they may have just lost one themselves!

By Nancy & Mike Pfeifer, Tim & Cindy McGray

CR SO

80 No Argument with Andy

Author and TV broadcaster Andy Kendeigh writes in his 208-page book *The Best Wisconsin Sports Arguments about the Green Bay Packers.* "If there's one team that unifies the state of Wisconsin, it's the Green Bay Packers. Churches schedule masses around Packers games. College basketball schedules have been reworked so they avoid competing with Packer games. The Packers are always the biggest sports story, week in and week out, even during the off-season. Any television news director in Wisconsin will tell you that there are two things that dominate news coverage in the state: the weather and the Green Bay Packers." Andy will get no argument from us.

He also has some very interesting numbers to share about the team and the town. "Green Bay, Wisconsin (population 102,313) is the smallest market in big-time sports. It's the one city in America where there's a unified, no-doubt-about-it, top dog in town. It's the Packers, 24/7, 365 days a year. When the Packers lose, those next mornings are a cold right hook to the face."

Here's another interesting point. "The Packers have the unique distinction of not having an owner. The fans own the team. Currently, 112,088 people (representing 4,750,936 shares) own the Green Bay Packers. The last stock offering came in 1997-1998, when the Packers raised $24 million by adding 105,989 shareholders at $20 a share."

Those sports franchises that have a hard time selling out will really be scratching their heads in amazement and gasping for air with envy when they read this. "Lambeau Field had been sold out since 1960. Would you believe 83,881 Packers fans remain on the waiting list? That means there are more fans on the waiting list to sit in Lambeau Field than there are actually sitting in Lambeau Field on game day. (Capacity 72,928)

How about some fun Packer trivia from Andy? Here's a great scenario and an even better question he posed in his work. "Two players define the franchise: Bart Starr and Brett Favre, both quarterbacks, both Hall of Famers, and both strangely successful playing in Wisconsin's elements. Each played 16 seasons in "Titletown." Between them, they won six NFL championships and four NFL MVP Awards. So if you had one game to win it for you, who would you choose number 15 or number 4?" We'll give you a moment to ponder it.

Andy's take is this. "My answer is Bart Starr. He was simply more consistent in big games. He won 9 of the 10 postseason games he played in. Favre was an above-average quarterback in the playoffs, finishing his Packers career with a 12-10 postseason record, but with him you never knew what you were going to get. For every play that he made you'd say, 'How did he do that?' there was also one that made you groan, 'How could he do that?' Favre is, without question, the most entertaining quarterback I have ever seen, but if I needed one quarterback to win one game, I'd choose Bart Starr."

Now wasn't that fun? Andy Kendeigh has spent a lot of time in his TV job in Milwaukee around the green-and-gold. Here's one of his favorite stories.

Winfred "Coop" Cooper's favorite football player is Donald Driver. He wears number 80 to prove it. It didn't matter that Coop went to high school in Elgin, IL, Bears country. Coop was a happy-go-lucky senior wide receiver. He showed up for practice on time, loved the games and, most importantly, loved football.

Coop played on Elgin's junior varsity team where, for the most part, he warmed the bench. He had never caught a pass in a game and didn't catch many in practice either. That all changed on September 12, 2009, in a game against Lake Park High School.

One of Lake Park's coaches, Nana Agyeman, noticed Coop.

"I went to talk to one of Elgin's assistant coaches at half time. 'If you want to throw the ball to number 80, just let us know.' The Elgin coaches agreed to put Cooper in. Lake Park then signaled each other by calling out, 'Driver! Driver! Driver!'" Agyeman remembers.

On the second play of the third quarter, Coop's number was called. He made his hero proud. He ran a perfect pattern, turned and reeled in the pass. The defenders were originally going to bring him down, but the two Lake Park defensive backs called an audible.

"He actually caught the ball. We had been told he probably wouldn't catch it, so when he did, I just kind of stopped. I just had to give him the touchdown because it was an amazing thing he did. I thought he really deserved it. I wanted to go down to the end zone and give him a high five, but he bolted away before I could," remembers Lake Park defensive back Daniel Henry.

Coop was thrilled to finally get into the end zone.

"It feels awesome, it feels awesome," was all Coop could say.

"Seeing him score that touchdown put the biggest smile on my face," said Lake Park defensive back Mike Schenone. "I looked over at Dan and I saw the same smile on his face. What a great feeling!"

His father, Winfried Cooper, Sr., was blown away.

"For me, it's the greatest feeling in the world. I've only seen him play a few times, and I've never seen him score a touchdown. It was the best feeling in the world for him, and for me," acknowledged the elder Cooper.

The story doesn't end there. Word of the "touchdown kid" traveled fast and far, 217 miles to be exact, all the way to Green Bay, Wisconsin.

When Donald Driver heard the news, he went on-line to YouTube to watch Coop's touchdown. Then he sent a video message along with a Milwaukee television reporter who would document Coop's story.

"I take my hat off to him. When he took off, he was gone. I think I might have to go down there and race him in the 40 to see if I can still beat him. He looked good, really good," Driver said.

You might be wondering what made Coop, or his touchdown reception, so special. There's nothing terribly inspirational, per se, about a high school football player who scores for his team. Why did Coop capture the attention of a pro-ball player? The answer is a simple one. Coop is autistic.

Winfred Cooper was moved to tears watching the message from his hero. Driver sent along an autographed hat and photo and one of his children's books. It was a day the young man will never forget, but neither will Driver. Inspiration is truly a two-way street.

You get no arguments, Andy. Donald Driver and the Green Bay Packers are a great bunch. Where else in professional sports can you find 75,00 people waiting to pay seat license fees and a good chunk of change for season tickets? Not only are the Packers a very special team, but Winfred Cooper is one special young man, even if does live in Bears country.

By Steve Rose

CR SO

81 Tim's Letter to Lombardi

Tim Hanna would memorize each Green Bay Packer roster before the start of every season. He would get to know the player, his number, where he went to school, everything. In the fall of 1965, Tim had a whale of an idea. He would write to Coach Lombardi to personally request the roster for that year's team. You have to admire the faith of a child, but clearly Tim didn't understand who Vince Lombardi was, or that with this man's work load the chances of Mr. Lombardi writing back were about the same as getting hit by lightning. Actually, the chance of getting hit by lightning might be greater!

Undaunted by such obvious road blocks to success, Tim wrote.

Dear Mr. Lombardi,

I am 8 years old and a big fan of the Packers. Could you please send me a roster so that I could begin memorizing the players and all their information? Thank you and good luck to

172

you this year.

Your friend,

Tim Hanna

Wouldn't you think that little Timmy would have to wait till Hades had frozen over, or for the Cubs to win a World Series, before he could expect a letter from Vince Lombardi? Not so. A few days later he got a typewritten letter postmarked from Green Bay.

Dear Tim,

   Thanks for your letter. You'll see that I have enclosed the roster for this coming season. Thank you for your interest and thanks for your well wishes.

Sincerely,

Coach Lombardi

Little Tim's faith was as strong as ever and he would strike green-and-gold one more time before the year was out. Each year, Coach Lombardi made his expectations clear to his players, expectations to be filled both on and off the field. One such off-the-field requirement was that the players were expected to go into the community and perform acts of kindness and service. One such involvement was for several of the players to attend the annual Trinity Lutheran Father & Son banquet. Tim and his father, Miles, attended the one in the winter of 1965. The Master of Ceremonies had a little contest.

"If anyone here can tell me who Packer #81 is, he'll get his picture taken with Ron Kostelnik," the commentator declared.

"That's Marv Fleming!" shouted Tim.

Within moments Tim was standing next to the tall defensive lineman getting his picture taken with one of his heroes.

"I was just telling Ron's daughter, Laura (who lives in Appleton), I had a really cool picture of her dad, taken in 1965," Tim told me. (Ron died in January 1993.)

Tim remembers his father taking him to another signing at Gibson Chevrolet, where two more of his favorite players, Don Chandler and Bart Starr, were going to be. He waited in line for what seemed like forever, but he did manage to get their autographs.

"Mr. Chandler, that was an awesome 90-yard punt you had this season," Tim mentioned to one of his Packer heroes.

"Thank you, Son," Chandler replied, clearly impressed with the young man's memory for detail.

Tim is currently the mayor of Appleton, WI. His story epitomizes the hearts of so many little boys who fondly follow the lives and careers of their beloved Packers. Tim's example of having faith in your dreams, and asking for what others may not, is enviable. It's a faith that has borne fruit. After all, he's got a letter from one Vincent T. Lombardi as proof.

By Steve Rose with memories from Tim Hanna

ଔ ଇ

82 Jersey, a Reminder of What Matters

Sometimes you find the most interesting items when cleaning out a closet. Recently, while going through my own I found, in the bottom of one of those plastic totes buried underneath sweatshirts and swimsuits no longer worn, an autographed Don Beebe jersey.

Holding it up brought back many fond memories, not just of 1997, when the Packers finally won the Super Bowl, but also of Beebe himself and what his jersey meant to me. I remember how my then finance (now husband) had traveled all the way from Manitowoc to the Fox River Mall in Appleton by himself to purchase the jersey as a surprise birthday gift. (I don't think he's been there since, by himself at least, even though we've lived in Appleton for more than a decade.)

This was no off-the-shelf jersey. Mine had been autographed. Back in the late 90s, it seemed as if every Packer had his own TV show, including Beebe. Joe arranged for us to get tickets to one of his shows. I can't recall who his guest was other than it was another Packer. It was at that show that Joe got the jersey autographed for me.

Holding that jersey reminded me of our young, fresh love for one another, the kind of love that makes you want to do everything you can for that other person, even if it involves driving an hour to a mall to buy a surprise gift for her. Now that we're married and have two young children, seeing that jersey again recalled to memory what a special love we shared then, and continue to share today.

I'm sure you're wondering, "Why a Beebe jersey? Wouldn't a Favre, Brooks, Freeman or another big "star's" jersey be a better choice?" Perhaps. But for me, Beebe was a role model, and Joe understood that. Before joining the Packers as a receiver, Beebe played for the Buffalo Bills. Every devoted football fan knows the Buffalo Bills of the 1990s lost four Super Bowls. In one of those games against Dallas, Beebe showed incredible persistence as he ran down and knocked the ball out of the hands of Leon Lett before he reached the end zone in spite of the fact that the Bills were down by three touchdowns. What an act of unwavering commitment.

At the same time that Beebe was achieving his goal of winning a Super Bowl ring as a Packer, I was facing some struggles in my own life. Beebe became a role model of sorts. The way he kept trying even when the odds were against him made me keep trying to achieve my own personal goals.

I held up the jersey once again and looked at it fondly before nicely folding it and putting it back in the bin. I doubt I'll ever wear it again, but it will always be a reminder of two things – the specialness of young love and the importance of persevering to follow your dreams.

By MaryBeth Matzek

❧ ❧

MaryBeth's Don Beebe jersey

175

83 For the Love of Brett

Marilyn Rohr has always considered herself a Packer fan, but when Brett Favre came to the Packers, she fell in love with his enthusiasm and love for the game. She was lucky enough to purchase an autographed copy of the photo that was taken of the game Brett played on December 22, 2003. The picture holds a special place in her heart because it represents Brett's willingness to play the game for his father, who had passed away only a day before.

In fact, the picture has come to mean so much to Marilyn that she replaced the family picture above her sofa, which had been there for years, with Brett's autographed picture! Initially, her family was surprised by the switch, but it's now come to be a family joke.

"We all thought it was odd that she would have such a love for a man that was young enough to be our brother, but we realized in time that she was genuinely attracted to his love of the game," Barb Marksman, Marilyn's daughter, admitted.

What could be said of Marilyn's response at hearing that the man she so loved and admired was going to leave the Packers?

"Mom actually called me at work and interrupted me while I was with a customer to tell me that Brett was leaving the Packers. She was heartbroken," remarked Barb.

While on a vacation in Mississippi, Marilyn and her husband Florian visited Brett's high school in Kiln. They had a picture taken of themselves standing next to his statue. They got to see where it all began for the man that she holds so dear.

Marilyn makes no apologies for her devotion to No. 4. She freely admits she considers herself to be blessed to have a signed picture of the man she believes epitomizes true passion for his game.

By Steve Rose with memories from Barb Marksman

CR SO

84 Tampa Bay Brats

Mad Dog & Merrill are two very well-known, well-traveled Packer fans who've never met a bratwurst they didn't like to grill. Let me point out that these boys are not amateurs. They actually grill for a living, and have been crisscrossing the nation doing so for nearly 30 years now.

According to Gary Merrill, all of their travels have proven one thing to be constant.

"The Packer fans from Wisconsin are amazing. They'll follow their team anywhere during the season, and there are more Packer fans in other cities than you might have thought. Bar owners in the cities where we're invited sponsor 'Packer Nights' or afternoon tailgate parties, depending on the time of the game," he pointed out.

One of those locations is Tampa, FL. It should come as no big surprise that there's an overwhelming number of snowbirds who love to fly south in December for a game. There are a variety of groups in other cities all over the country featuring Packer establishments, places where die-hard fans can stop to watch a game and feel like they're back home (except for the snow). Gary vividly recalls one visit to Florida in October of '92. He remembers it because the main dish nearly didn't make it to the tailgate party on time.

We were being hosted by one of the local bars. We usually in the night before to make all the arrangements. The brats were scheduled to arrive bright and early the next morning so we could cook them up for the crowd by the time they arrived for the "feeding frenzy" at around 11a.m.," he recalled.

Gary and his partner Mad Dog arrived at the venue at 7 a.m. Armed with all their utensils, the large eight-foot grills were filled with coals and lit in preparation to cook the meaty treats for the Packer faithful. Also on hand were about 25 volunteers who would help pull off this affair to feed no less than two-thousand mouths, including the local Mayor. Packer legend Ray Nitschke was to be in attendance to entertain and sign autographs.

"The plan we had agreed on the night before was that the bar owner, who was keeping the brats chilled at his establishment, was going to bring them to the venue that morning. It got to be 8 – 8:30'ish, and still no brats. There were about a thousand people waiting outside the gate," said Merrill.

Another hour passed. Gary became more than concerned. There were still no brats, and the crowd outside the gates continued to grow.

"It's after 10 a.m. and now I'm really worried, and I'm wondering, 'What the heck has gone wrong?' And then, off in the distance, I see a truck coming across the lot. At approximately 10:40 a.m. the bar owner arrived, brats in tow. He never said a word about why he was late, and I never asked. We got those brats on the grill and actually had them ready by 11."

Gary then makes a key observation.

"You know, as passionate and as over the top as Packer fans can be, I have to tell you, I truly believe if the brats had not arrived, the crowd would have remained calm and civil. I really do believe that. Packer fans have a reputation for being rowdy folks, and some are, but I was never really nervous about the situation."

That said, whether it be Tampa, Dallas or Phoenix, Mad Dog & Merrill hope the brats arrive on time so they can feed the green-and-gold faithful, some of whom may have been in the crowd that nearly went hungry in Tampa in 1992.

By Steve Rose with memories from Gary Merrill

ભ જ

85 Max

Rob Hamilton fought and lost friends in the Vietnam War. He's also lived long enough to bury many relatives, including his father. Nothing, however, has affected him as deeply as the loss of his close friend, Max McGee, who died after falling off the roof of his home in Deephaven, MN, October 20, 2007.

Hamilton was introduced to Max in 1992. Before then, he only knew

McGee from his Packer days. Rob was considerably younger than the former NFL star. Once introductions were made, right up until that day in 2007, Rob and Max spent almost every morning at the Original Pancake House. They'd do crossword puzzles together over breakfast, sometimes staying until 10 or 11 a.m., doing whatever it took to get them done.

"The first day we had breakfast I asked Max if he was the MVP of Super Bowl I. Without missing a beat he said, 'I was, but they gave the car to Bart,'" laughed Rob upon remembering that line.

McGee was known to many as the guy who stayed out beyond curfew the night before the first Super Bowl and the one who gave Lombardi fits. Underneath that person was a softhearted gentleman who, once he became a father to two sons, was changed forever, according to Rob.

Maxie, who has Down Syndrome, and Dallas, diagnosed with Juvenile Diabetes, changed their father's life in many ways. Make no mistake. Max McGee was a quality man before they were born, but the best of Max surfaced after they were born.

Jerry Kramer, Max's former teammate and business partner in the Left Guard, was tremendously upset when he heard the news of his friend's death.

"I don't know what the h*** Max was doing up on that roof. I remember him telling me in the early '90s that he was selling his place in Arizona so he could be back in Minneapolis to be a father to his boys. I was so proud of the father that Max had become," Kramer said.

Today, Rob and the McGee brothers remain pretty tight.

Maxie is my buddy. He'll spend lots of time with me when I'm in the area. Dallas is currently at DePaul University and is in good health. He looks just like his father's high school picture. Dallas was a sweet kid with a great smile who has grown into a fine young man and a good friend," claimed Hamilton.

The elder McGee had been recently diagnosed with the early onset of Alzheimers. Rob and the other breakfast buddies knew that, at some point, they'd need to do all the driving, transporting Max to and from breakfast, and generally keep a closer eye on him, but that stage never came. The loss of McGee happened so unexpectedly. That part still irks Hamilton.

"We had breakfast that morning of October 20. I said goodbye to him at 10, and by 6 o'clock that same day we got the word that he had died. I've never gotten over losing him, and I never will."

McGee was a great player, businessman, husband, and father. He was a radio broadcaster for almost 20 years for the team he played for in Green Bay.

"Max had an incredible way of making you feel like you were his best friend. When Max introduced you to someone, it gave you instant credibility," Rob remembered.

Rob was always amazed that, even though he wasn't an athlete or golfer like his friend, Max still hung around with him.

"I didn't play football, golf, or any sports, for that matter. I'm fairly certain he kept me around to help him with the crossword puzzles," laughed Hamilton.

It's obvious by Rob's voice when he speaks about his friend that the loss will leave a hole in his heart, not unlike the hole that also exists for his sons, the Packer nation, the community and the boys and staff at the Original Pancake House in Minneapolis.

By Steve Rose with memories from Rob Hamilton

ल्ष ≥

86 Antonio's Trash is Another's Treasure

In the 1990's, my brother Gary Long and I were partners in our family business, A-1 Moving & Storage. Mom and Dad, then Gary and I, had been moving people in Northeast Wisconsin for over 35 years.

Flash back with me to the week before Super Bowl XXXI. No doubt, people believe the players were just practicing, practicing, practicing before the big game, but we forget that the players also have to take care of the details of daily life.

Now, as then, many of the players have apartments in Green Bay just for the season. Then they head back home once the season is over. It might interest you to know that the Packer players are a pretty superstitious bunch. They never make arrangements for the move from their apartments back to their hometowns until their season is officially over.

In the years before 1995 and 1996, we often got calls all day on the Monday after the Packers were eliminated from the playoffs. Oftentimes, that was even before the playoffs were started. In January of 1997, however, the players called us the week before their last game, because they knew it would truly be their last game, the Super Bowl. They knew that by the following Monday morning, their season would be over.

It was such great fun to take calls that week and speak with LeRoy Butler, Antonio Freeman, Dorsey Levens, Craig Newsome, Terry Mickens and Edgar Bennett, each asking about moving the week after the game. They were calling us from sunny New Orleans, while we were back in the frozen tundra of Green Bay, still in football frenzy!

The Friday night after the Super Bowl, Antonio Freeman flew into town. On Saturday morning, he had about five hours to clear out his entire apartment before flying back out. He hadn't been there much in the weeks prior, so with all the excitement of the playoffs, he had done very little, if any, sorting or packing for the move.

When we got there, I (naturally) assigned myself to supervise the move. Some of our crew started in the kitchen. Others started in the living room. I found myself in the office with Antonio. We were sorting through a variety of things he no longer wanted, and throwing them in the trash. At one point, as I held the garbage bag open for him, Antonio threw away some old clothes and a football.

"Antonio," I gasped in disbelief. "Wait! You've just won the Super Bowl! If you just sign that football, I could give it to a charity and they could make good money from what you're tossing into the trash!"

He shook his head and chuckled. I tossed the ball back to him, and then gave him my marker for labeling boxes. He signed the football with a flourish.

"There you go," he said, tossing the ball right back to me.

Rather than going into the trash, the football went, instead, to Make-a-Wish for a raffle. And, as I tell my friends, I had the opportunity to play catch with Antonio Freeman!

By Jean Long Manteufel

CR ЕО

87 Happy 14ᵗʰ "Brooksday"

So far, I've celebrated 25 birthdays in my lifetime. These birthdays have often involved dinners out to my favorite restaurants and Grandma Yodi's delicious chocolate cake. A recent birthday even included a proposal and an engagement ring! Over the years I've received many cherished gifts on February 24th. There is one birthday, however, that is vivid in my mind, even 11 years later.

My dad was a busy man. Besides working a great deal, he was an Ironman athlete who was constantly training for his next race. He'd often leave for work well before I woke up for school and return home just in time for a quick dinner before a bike ride. On Feb. 24, 1999, (a Wednesday) I walked downstairs for breakfast and found him sitting in the kitchen.

"Happy Birthday! I've got a surprise for you today!" he said cheerfully to me.

Dad explained that he called my school and reported me "sick" so we could spend the day together instead. This news floored me. The thought of not only missing school, but spending time with Dad, immediately put me in a good mood.

As I went upstairs to get dressed for our mysterious day, Dad told me that I may want to wear Packer gear. Something about the tone of his voice combined with the suggestion of Packer gear caused my heart to race as I put on my Robert Brooks jersey. I was, like all true Wisconsinites, a huge Packer fan and when it came to #87 I was a die-hard supporter. I absolutely loved watching the Packers every Sunday, and cheered along with my family as Brooks perfected the Lambeau Leap.

Dad and I didn't get to spend much time alone together (I am the oldest of three girls. Most of the time spent with Dad was shared time with my younger sisters.) I cherished the ride on 41 North with him and having him all to myself. LFO played on the radio, and Dad attempted to sing along with me as he drove. I tried to get information from Dad about our mystery destination. After driving for about 20 minutes he finally gave in and responded to me with a huge grin, "We're going to go visit Robert. You know, Robert Brooks. That wide receiver for the Packers that you're obsessed with."

At that point, I knew Dad had to be teasing me. He was probably driving me to an unknown destination where there would be a picture of Robert Brooks. There was no way that Dad could have lined up a meeting with him. He wouldn't even be in Green Bay during the off-season, right? Maybe he had a connection. Dad did seem to be constantly bumping into people he knew and he was friends with everyone. Perhaps someone arranged something!

As we continued to drive, Dad exited the highway near residential neighborhoods. My mind was racing. What was he up to? As we sat at a stop light Dad confidently declared again that we were going to Robert Brooks' house. We drove into a subdivision and Dad slowly starting making his way through the neighborhood.

We rounded a corner and Dad said, "Well, we're here!"

The look on my face must have been priceless because Dad laughed and explained that he didn't have a way for me to meet Brooks for my birthday, but at least I could see where he lived.

The beauty of the Green Bay Packers is that they are a professional sports organization that is truly part of the community. Dad explained that he wanted me to see the "real person" side of Robert Brooks. He explained that there was a difference between the Packers and other NFL teams. Fans in other cities simply don't have the hometown connection that Packer fans have with their organization. I wouldn't truly understand or appreciate the reality of his explanation until I grew up and lived in Viking territory for seven years.

I stared at Brooks' house in awe. The quiet subdivision wasn't quite what I had imagined. I tried to visualize him coming home from Packer practices and games and relaxing just like everyone else living in the Green Bay area. Even though I knew Brooks was in Arizona for the off season, my heart beat faster with even the possibility that my favorite athlete may walk out the front door at any second.

Dad and I sat silently for a few moments as I tried to comprehend the event that had just unfolded. Seeing where Robert Brooks lived only increased my love for #87. We could have gone right back to Neenah at that point and I would have been more than satisfied with my 14th birthday.

But there was more! We spent the rest of the day together at the Packer

Hall of Fame. I was totally energized and beyond excited to be surrounded by all that was Packer. Dad even embraced my teenage enthusiasm (and dorkiness!) and posed with me for pictures with the life size cut-outs of Butler and Favre. We practiced kicking game-winning field goals and learned some more of the history of our treasured Packers.

My 14th birthday present that year wasn't an item that I could carry with me. Instead, it was a cherished memory that would stay with me forever. One thing I've learned in my first two years of teaching 8th grade is that while 14-year olds definitely feel gratitude, they do not always verbalize it. So, in case I didn't tell you Dad...thank you for the best birthday present of all.

The significance of my 14th birthday has only grown each year since then. I never would have guessed that I would only spend one more birthday with my dad. To be honest, I don't even remember my 15th birthday.

A year and a half after my "Brooksday" adventure, Steve Levine, my dad, my hero, and the man behind my most memorable birthday, lost his battle with cancer. I spent 15 short years with him. Fifteen birthdays that will last a lifetime, all important, each priceless, but this one will remain green and gold in my heart forever.

By Jen (Levine) Moe

Jennifer (LeVine) Moe with her father, Steve LeVine

184

88 Not a Fair Weather Fan

I was born and raised a Green Bay Packer fan, so I've seen plenty of great moments in Packer history. As a youngster, our family would take the annual trip to a Packer pre-season practice and we'd stay in a hotel with a swimming pool. We even got to go to Bay Beach Amusement Park the next day. I was six, maybe seven years old, walking up to players like Ray Nitschke, Jerry Kramer, Fuzzy Thurston, and Willie Wood to ask for an autograph. After all, who's going to turn down a little buzz-cut haired kid with a Bart Starr jersey on? I remember my small fingers curled around the links in the fence, watching intently as Vince Lombardi barked at his players. Little did I know then that this man would be perhaps the greatest football coach to ever walk the planet.

My Packer game experiences are nothing short of bizarre. In 1985, as a junior at UW-Oshkosh, deciding to go home for a weekend meant just a short 20-minute trip back to Fond du Lac. One Saturday night, my friend Marc Curcurio asked me to go with him to the Packer game the next day. I jumped at the opportunity and agreed to be his co-pilot.

Sunday morning we awoke to nearly 12 inches of snow, and it was still coming down by the bucket loads. Marc arrived on time for our 9 a.m. departure. My mother thought we were absolutely insane for even considering a drive to Green Bay in such horrible road conditions. She was right. (Moms usually are.) What in the world could possess two college-aged students to drive 60 miles in a blizzard? The answer was simple – the Green Bay Packers.

It took us well over two hours to get to Green Bay as highway traffic was condensed from two lanes down to one. Lambeau Field parking lot was only one- third full and the piles of plowed snow looked like the Grand Tetons. Tailgating was more than adventurous given that it was impossible to keep our grill lit. It was an incredible sight to enter the stadium and see only 19,856 fans. It was the smallest crowd recorded in Lambeau history.

There was a carnival-like atmosphere. Adults regressed into little kids, replete with all of the childish shenanigans you'd expect like throwing snowballs at each other and sliding down the stairs on their rear ends.

Another four to five inches fell during the game itself, but we barely noticed. The Packers were absolutely dominating the Tampa Bay Bucs 21-0, and had gained an incredible 512 total yards in spite of the horrid conditions. The Packer defense bordered on the miraculous, holding the Bucs to 65 total yards in Steve Young's second game with Tampa Bay.

During a bathroom break, I ran into my college roommate, a native of Green Bay. He graciously invited us to stay at his place should we end up having trouble getting back on the roads after the game. Forget the roads! We could barely get out of the parking lot! So, we took him up on his offer. Needless to say, we didn't make it back to Oshkosh for Monday's classes, but I don't remember any of us losing much sleep over that fact.

Now, you might be tempted to chalk up this experience to youthful indiscretion and a lack of the wisdom that comes with more maturity, all of which would be true. Unfortunately, I wouldn't be able to use that as an excuse 15 years later.

It was November 6, 2000. Once again we stumbled upon some Packer tickets. Our good friends and neighbors, Mark and Jamie Birschbach, had two extra tickets for the Monday night game against rival Minnesota. The weather that day was rainy and cold. It almost made us wish we had stayed home to watch it from the comfort of our nice warm living room…almost. But die-hard Packer fans brave the elements, no matter what they are, and brave the weather we did! We managed to keep a grill going just long enough to cook up a few brats before the game, and then decked ourselves in heavy-duty rain gear as if it were armor and we were like soldiers about to go into battle.

We were barely into the first quarter, and already we were soggy, totally soaked and cold, but the view was excellent from our seats on the 10-yard line about 20 rows up. The Packers appeared to be doomed with only seven seconds left in the game when Viking kicker Gary Anderson lined up for a 32-yard field goal with the score tied 20-20. Anderson pushed the field goal wide. The Pack came back to life as the game went into overtime where we witnessed perhaps one of the most amazing catches in NFL history.

Faced with a 3rd and four from the Minnesota 43-yard line, Brett Favre dropped back and unloaded a bomb down field to Antonio Freeman. Viking Chris Dishman tipped the pass twice. Freeman dove for the ball and miraculously corralled it after it caromed off his shoulder and facemask. Freeman instantly jumped to his feet and raced to the end zone for the game-winning touchdown. The officials reviewed the play. We all held our breaths. After a short delay, the referee made the call. Touchdown! The crowd of 60,000 people, all of them cold, wet and exhausted from cheering, hollering and side-line reffing, went berserk. We all danced in the freezing rain like a bunch of college kids as the song YMCA blared over the PA system.

Fast forward to January 12, 2008. The Packers were hosting their former coach Mike Holmgren and his Seattle Seahawks in the second round of the NFC playoffs.

It was an incredibly cold and blustery afternoon. We tailgated at the K-Mart parking lot right next to the stadium. Caravans of cars, buses, and mobile homes filled the lot for the 3 p.m. game. It's an amazing experience to sit back and observe the cultural phenomenon that takes place at these games. Packer fans from across the state and beyond, many of whom are total strangers to one another, mingle and socialize with each other as if everyone's at a family reunion.

The Packers spotted the Seahawks an early 14-0 lead in the first quarter, but the green and gold would storm back hard and heavy. Snow storm back, that is! The snow started to fly, and so did the Packers. By the second quarter, the field was blanketed with heavy snow and, true to form, the Packer fans loved every minute of it. The snow storm seemed to propel the Packers to an unbelievable surge that led to a 42-20 comeback and the NFC championship game.

Who, other than a true, never-say-die Packer backer, would have thought?

By Mark Peterson

ᘓ ᘔ

89 I Like the Old Packers Myself

My memories of the Green Bay Packers go back to the 1950s, when I was ten to twelve years of age, listening to the radio with my dad on a Sunday afternoon, either in the car or sitting in the back yard. That was before the glory years, but I still recall the names: Floyd "Breezy" Reid at halfback, Howard Ferguson at fullback, and both Tobin Rote and Vito "Babe" Parilli, who shared quarterback duty in the mid-fifties.

The call on the radio still echoes in my ears: "The 'give' is to Ferguson, off left tackle for three, no make that four yards. And it's now third down and two for the Packers at the Chicago Bears' 46 yard line."

Then, of course, we suffered through the horrible year of 1958, with Scooter McLean coaching the team for that year alone. The Packers record was 1-10-1. I actually got to watch a game at the new City Stadium (later renamed Lambeau Field) that same year. The Packers were humiliated the day I went, by an embarrassing 38-0 score.

Enter Vince Lombardi. I don't think I missed a single game on either TV or radio for the next 11 years.

We saw 1959 become a turn-around year under Lombardi, and what followed were eight near-miraculous years with him. I loved, (and sometimes agonized over) every exciting minute.

I like the "old Packers." They played a different kind of football compared with today's game. The Pack defiantly ran more than passed, and they dared their opponents to try to stop them. Jim Taylor and Paul Hornung were a dangerous duo. Taylor often went inside, running over linebackers, while Hornung went outside, using the famed Green Bay Packer sweep, following guards Jerry Kramer and Fuzzy Thurston. Forrest Gregg may have been the best offensive tackle/pass protector in team history. As a result, more running meant the games went more quickly.

When passing was needed, Bart Starr could be deadly accurate, although, in my opinion, he was also a bit "brittle." Famed TV announcer Ray Scott would state it succinctly: "Starr…Dowler…touchdown!" That was all the verbalism necessary.

On defense those "old" Packers had Dave "Hawg" Hanner and Willie Davis up front, Ray Nitschke at middle linebacker, as well as Willie Wood and Bob Jeter in the secondary. The 1962 version of that team finished 13-1, beating the Giants for the second year in a row for the NFL title. The one loss, to the Lions, ruined our Thanksgiving dinners that year, as Alex Karras and his mates were all over Bart Starr, manhandling our Packers convincingly.

I like the "old Packers" because their boss, Vince Lombardi, ruled the team. I like the "old Packers" because they didn't show off or do ridiculous dances when they made a good play. I like the "old Packers" because the players had long-lasting loyalties to the city, state, and fans. I like the "old Packers" because they brought a fame and notoriety to small town Green Bay and to all of us who grew up or lived in small-town USA. It was a notoriety we had never enjoyed before, not even in the glory days of the Milwaukee Braves, because the Braves were, after all, "big city."

Call me crazy. Call me old fashioned. I can't help myself. Just give me the "good old days."

By Jim Vollmer, former CHS faculty/coach, 1966-2004

CR SO

90 The Packers Can Thank Q-90FM

Radio station Q-90FM, an up-tempo Christian-music formatted listener-supported signal in Green Bay, has played a significant role in the lives of many notable players since 1993. Those call letters may sound familiar to you. I did a radio show, Time Out, hosted with Ken Ruettgers, Don Beebe and John Michels from 1994 through early 1997. It was an opportunity for listeners to get a peek into the lives of some of their Packer heroes, as well as into their lives of faith.

This book would not have been complete without input from my former boss and current Director of Broadcast Operations of the "Q," Jim "Kid" Raider. A recent visit with him at their new studio included a quick tour, which concluded with our arrival in the station's prayer room where we did the interview. I was anxious to hear his memories of those special days when Kenny and the fellows would come in to share how the Lord was helping them deal with their lives, both on and off the field.

Jim prayed and then he began to reminisce.

"Jim, what do you remember from those times when we did the show?"

"Aw, man. Getting to know Ken, Reggie and Sara (White), Bryce

(Paup), Mark Brunnell, 'Beebs' (Don Beebe), John (Michels), those were great times."

"When's the last time you've seen any of the guys?" I quizzed.

"Actually, John came to my wedding in '97. John and Melissa got married in February and I got married in June. As you know, Steve, John is such a great guy. He really helped the station a lot."

Jim's assessment was mine as well. John's influence helped me secure The Leap of Faith TV show, which ran on FOX 11 WLUK in Green Bay from 1998 to 1999. Most everyone from Green Bay knows that Packer players can open doors of opportunity that might otherwise be closed to us 'mere mortals.' I was, and always will be, grateful for the help that John provided.

But I digress.

"I remember the day in '96 when Deanna Favre called to match a pledge (Q90FM is listener supported). We were going to lose a substantial amount of money unless someone matched the challenge, so she and Brett did. That was cool, but it was an even greater blessing to know they were listeners. Oh, so were several other players, like Alan Rossum, Billy Schroeder, Doug Pederson and Matt Hasselback," he recalled.

"Of course, Reggie and Sara White were faithful listeners and helpful contributors. Remember, Steve, Reggie had 'Big Dog' records, and we used to play some of his artists."

That was a fact I had forgotten. Jim continued without missing a beat.

"The Whites became 'day sponsors' on their kids' (Jeremy and Jecoliah) birthdays. As a matter of fact, about a month before Reggie died, I saw Sara and she said, 'I still listen to you guys on-line' which really blessed me."

Kid paused just long enough to take a breath before continuing.

"Ryan Longwell loved listening to the Q and he and Sarah were great supporters. I believe he may still listen on-line."

"Kid, how long are you planning to stay here at Q-90?" I quizzed.

"I tell people 'you'll have to talk to my travel agent,'" he chuckled, pointing toward heaven.

Before we broke up our one-hour trip down memory lane, Kid brought up the name of one of the station's fans, a young man named Aaron Rodgers. Anyone who knows anything about him will not be surprised to know that he is always sharing about his faith in Jesus Christ. It was, for me, the perfect close to a great interview.

I gave Jim a hug at the door as we exchanged goodbyes. A hundred years from now, there are a lot of aspects about what any of us have done that won't matter, but there's a radio station in Green Bay whose listeners work at 1265 Lombardi Avenue. Their faith is being encouraged, helping them to become stronger believers and better people. For that, the Packers can thank Q-90FM.

By Steve Rose with memories from Jim "Kid" Raider

CR SO

91 When Johnny Got Off the Bus

My first experience with the Packers was in August of 1970. I was an eight-year-old on a bus trip with the Appleton Recreation Department. The plan was to spend some time riding bumper cars and having fun at Bay Beach, an amusement park in Green Bay. But I had come to Green Bay to go to see the "house that Curly built," and to watch the annual Packer Intra Squad game. I could barely contain my excitement.

"Man, this is going to be so great!" I blurted out to the person next to me on the bus.

"Yeah, I know. I can't wait," he chimed right back.

I had the same butterflies in my stomach that I'd get before a little league game or other competitions. What none of us were aware of was that there were some Labor issues going on between the players and the NFL. We had absolutely no understanding of it, nor did we care.

Having only seen the stadium on TV, my eyes widened to the size of saucers when our yellow bus pulled into the parking lot. Lambeau Field! I was awestruck.

"Wow, look at that!" was all that would come out of my mouth.

We got off the bus to be greeted by a few of my favorite green-and-gold warriors who were on what would turn out to be a four-day strike. Still holding their picket signs, we walked among them as if there wasn't a thing wrong.

I cordially and excitedly greeted them, one by one.

"Hey, Clarence, Jim, Gale, Mike, Fred and Lionel!"

"Wow, for a little guy, you're quite the Packer fan, aren't you?" Clarence remarked, impressed with the fact that I knew each of them by name.

"You bet I am!" I boasted, standing next to my heroes. I was like a kid in a candy store.

Unlike today, we didn't have camera phones, but I did have a piece of paper, so I feverishly got as many autographs as I could.

The enormity of the stadium left me virtually speechless for several minutes. Although the game was only an Intra Squad game with scabs, free agents and rookies, it didn't matter to me. I was in Lambeau Field watching my favorite team, well, in a manner of speaking. I especially remember focusing my attention on quarterback Frank Patrick and St. Norbert's own Larry Krause.

I'm much older now and I have been fortunate enough to have attended a few games over the years, but there's something to be said for experiencing Lambeau for the first time through the eyes of an idealistic eight-year-old Packer fan.

I'll never forget the night I spent at my Mecca, where I got to pay homage to Clarence Williams, Jim Carter, Gale Gillingham, Mike McCoy, Fred Carr, and Lionel Aldridge. It's the thing dreams are made of.

By John Leopold

CR SO

92 Packer Powers

My early football fan days consisted of watching pro football on TV and then playing pickup games with pals from the neighborhood afterword. My old "Bart Starr" football became well worn through my years as a boy growing up near Lodi, WI. Years later, I found myself having a deep appreciation for a number of players because of their Christian faith, including Reggie White. Little did I know that someday my life would be touched forever by the "Minister of Defense."

I had never personally experienced the power of a football star who took the time to help our family grasp the profound truth that God loved us and that even in the midst of a life-altering loss, God was working out His plan!

I come from a family of five boys, Doug Tom, John and Sam, all of whom are considerably older than me. Allow me to share a very personal family story. I hope it will give you some insight into what a remarkable man Reggie was.

It was a cold, foggy, February morning in 1996 when my brother Tom's boy was killed a car accident on Interstate 90/94. Needless to say, this was a very difficult and heartbreaking time for our family. Although our faith was strong, we were all so devastated. Tim was only 21 years old.

Shortly after the tragedy occurred, I met Steve Rose at a Fellowship of Christian Athletes event in Milwaukee. Reggie and Sara White were there, as well. I met Reggie in the hallway just before he spoke.

"Hi, Reggie. My name is Mike Powers." I extended my hand.

"Hi, Mike. It's nice to meet you," he said, as his large hand enveloped mine.

His talk was so encouraging. As I left that evening, an idea began to germinate in my soul. I decided to write Reggie a letter sharing the challenges our family was facing in trying to deal with Tim's untimely death. In the letter, I asked him if he would write to Tom to encourage him. Here it is.

March 17, 1996
Dear Tom:

I just wanted to write a note of encouragement. Your brother Mike told me about your son, Tim. Although I have been a father for only 9 years, I know how much your family loved your child. However, I don't know why he was taken from your family. But I do know God loves you and His love is there with you and your family. In times of trouble, He wants us to depend on Him. We go through so much on this earth for His sake. I have gone through a lot in my 34 years, but I have learned not to question God. I guess I am writing because you lost some precious jewel, just keep the memories and continue to serve God with all your heart and might.

Peace in Christ,

Reggie White

It was amazing how much better we all felt by simply receiving a short note of care and concern. When our family heard of Reggie's passing on the day after Christmas, 2004, we felt as if we had lost a part of our own family. We, in turn, sent a note to the White family hoping to encourage them just as Reggie had encouraged us.

When I see the Packers, I no longer see a football uniform or helmet of green and gold. I see so much more than that. I know our family has been only one of many families touched by the team and town in some way. We are grateful it was Reggie White who touched ours.

By Michael Powers

CR ED

Don Beebe and Mike Powers

93 The Day Ditka Won Packer Tickets

I am a die-hard Bears fan, but I have tremendous respect for Packer fans and the Packer organization. Steve Rose is a great friend of mine. We've known each other for nearly ten years. He, and the guys we play racquetball with, have given me my share of grief for my allegiance to the Bears. I confess I've dished out a generous portion of grief to them, as well, all in good fun.

Several years ago, after moving from Fond du Lac to Appleton, a half-hour south of Green Bay, I began to attend mostly Bear-Packers games at Lambeau Field. After only a few seasons, I realized that Packer fans were really decent, genuine folks. They're not the typical fair-weather fans you find in most other cities. They come to the game totally committed to cheering on their team. They show up wearing blaze orange and cheesehead hats in below-freezing temperatures and root for their team even in the midst of a losing season. Year after year, they fill up the seats, even late into the season, even after the team's been eliminated from the playoffs. Win or lose, it's always a sellout crowd.

The most memorable game I attended was on Christmas 2005 against my beloved Bears. What made it most special was that it was the first NFL game my son and I attended together. I had paid face value for two tickets, which I purchased from a local attorney. I also had entered a raffle at a company of a friend who was at a sports establishment when I called him. I was anxious to know if I had won, so I called over there.

"Have you guys drawn the ticket winners for the Packer-Bear game yet?"

"No, not yet, but we're going to in a bit," he replied.

"Tell you what. Why don't you put my name in the hat for another chance," I requested. It cost me another $10, but I had an idea.

"Put my nickname on the raffle ticket, will you?" I requested.

Well, guess who won two more tickets to that Christmas Packer-Bear game? I credit the good fortune to using my nickname. I only wish that I had been there when my name was called. Just imagine the lady, standing on top of the bar, giving notice of the winner with these words.

"Is Mike Ditka here? Mike Ditka, you've won the tickets!"

I'm told the lady was oblivious to who Mike Ditka was. Although a few of the patrons in the bar were initially a bit irritated, I was also told that more than a few smirked at my cleverness and the use of my nickname for some fun in Packerland.

At this juncture in my life, I'm single. Should I marry, it will probably be to a woman from the area who is a die-hard Packer fan. Hopefully, she won't wear blaze orange, or a cheesehead hat, and should we need one, a marriage counselor will accept emergency calls on Sunday afternoons.

Did I mention that the Bears won the game that I had won raffle tickets to? (Just had to get that in there!) Talk about lucky all the way around.

I continue to cheer for the Packers, except when they're up against the Bears, of course. If you're ever standing next to me at a Packer-Bear game, I hope you're one of those Packer fans I mentioned earlier…you know, the kind, polite, decent, and even tempered kind. I think we can all agree on one thing, at least. It just wouldn't be a good thing if a Packer fan beat up "Mike Ditka!"

By Mike "Ditka" Kreiman

94 Packer Cover Story

It was May 19, 2003. I had made a trip to Freedom- Freedom, WI that is. This small town is not far from the football Mecca of the world, Lambeau Field, home of the legendary Green Bay Packers. So it was hardly surprising that I had encountered a Packer fan that day.

I was sitting in the spacious lobby of Vista Marketing waiting to meet with its president, Connie Campbell, to talk business. It was a stunning facility and my eyes were taking it all in when a voice broke into my daydreaming.

"Can I offer you something to drink?"

"Thanks, but I'm doing okay," I said.

After a few minutes of silence, I initiated some more conversation with the young woman at the front desk.

"You look awfully busy," I said.

"I am, but I love my job!" she came back without hesitation.

"My name is Steve," as I extended my hand to shake hers.

"I'm Julie," she said, doing the same.

I guessed her to be about 20 years old.

"This is a great little town," I said, referring to Freedom, the home of the hometown Irish, the nickname of the high school just down the street. Their green and gold colors evoke respect from players and fans alike, but there's a "greater" green and gold in these parts.

"I understand it's a nice place to live, although I wouldn't know, since I only work here. Actually I drive down from Green Bay each day," she informed me.

Let me assure you that most of us in Wisconsin are well trained. When the city of Green Bay is mentioned, it's customary, proper, and expected to at least chat about the latest Packer news. However, I had another question first.

"In what part of Green Bay do you live, Julie?" I asked.

She went on to describe a part of the city with which I was quite familiar. From my years of working with and writing about the Packers, I recognized the general vicinity to which she was referring.

"Oh, you live not too far from my friend, Robert Brooks. So, you probably know that Brett Favre is over in that area, too."

"Sure do."

"Are you a big Packer fan?" I quizzed.

"You bet I am! We even go to a few home games from time to time. In fact, I was on the front cover of a Packer book one time."

"No kidding! Which one?" I asked.

"I think it was 'God's a Packer Fan' or something."

"Really?" I questioned, trying to be nonchalant. "Excuse me, Julie. I'll be right back."

I went to my car trunk, and returned to this young Packer fan in no less than a minute, holding a hardcover book. I pointed to the front cover photo that had a group of teenage kids on it.

"Which one is you, Julie?" I questioned holding it in front of her.

"This one right here," she pointed, beaming from ear to ear.

"This one is me," I pointed to STEVE ROSE at the bottom of the front cover. "I wrote it in 1996!"

By Steve Rose

95 Likable Lionel

Like most kids who grew up in Wisconsin during the '60s, I was glued to the television set Sunday after Sunday watching the Green Bay Packers. I knew all their names, all their numbers, and just about everything else about the green and gold. Some of my personal favorites were Bart Starr, Ray Nitschke, Jim Taylor, Paul Hornung and Lionel Aldridge.

I met Lionel when he was working as a sportscaster for WTMJ Channel 4 in Milwaukee. My journalism career was in its infancy. I was attending Marquette University J-School, working part-time at the Milwaukee Sentinel and doing freelance feature work in sports.

Lionel and Channel 4's Sports Director at the time, Hank Stoddard, would come downtown to a favorite watering hole for media types, Major Goolsby's. Sports Illustrated had dubbed Goolsby's the "liquid locker room." There was no more popular spot in town.

It didn't matter to Lionel that I was just starting out. He treated me as a peer. I still hold a great deal of admiration for him for that alone. He never made a big deal out of the fact that he was a Super Bowl champ or that he was a star on the rise as an analyst for the National Football League games on NBC. He was simply Lionel Aldridge, human being, and nice guy with no pretensions whatsoever.

Lionel didn't think of himself as a pioneer, though he most certainly was. I believe he was the first African-American to do network color commentary on pro football. He never flaunted his celebrity status, nor did he let any of that ego stuff get in the way of him being who he was.

One day, something inside his head just snapped. The mental illness that would haunt him for most of the rest of his days had seized control. Schizophrenia is an insidious disease that takes over the best part of far too many of our fellow man. Lionel fell through the cracks and dropped out of sight.

I saw him again late one night at Goolsby's, although it took me awhile to recognize him. He was an unshaven shell of his former self, not at all the 6-3, 254-pound guy I had known. He looked so troubled and after a couple of minutes he was gone. The next chapter in Lionel's saga

Pea Soup News and Notes...

Go to the website below if you would like to do any of the following...

* Order discounted, author-autographed copies of this or other Steve and Kathi Rose books
* If you have a Packer-related story that you would like to have considered for any future editions of *Pea Soup for the Packer Heart*
* If you would like to contact any of the contributors of stories in this book. We do ask you to respect their privacy and make those requests at the official website
* If you would like to have Steve or Kathi Rose or the "Pea Soup Pack of WI" come and do a benefit or other book signing near you

www.peasouppackerbook.com

Titletown Memories

If you like this book, you'll love the 30-minute Packer blast from the past radio show that pays tribute to former and current players who have graced the frozen tundra of Lambeau Field. Host Steve Rose guides listeners through flashbacks to the '60s, the Lombardi glory day heroes, all the way through to the memories from players today. A Packer fan is also featured on each segment to share green-and-gold nostalgia fun with Steve and the Packer. From the recognizable opening Packer theme to the close, "Packermaniacs" will be lost in the mystique that has enveloped the lives of those who've had the Packer experience. Give it a listen!

www.titletownmemoriesradio.com

was a victory every bit as important as winning pro football's top prize. He had gotten help and medication that, for a long time, brought him back from the edge of the precipice.

He was working at the post office and for the Alliance for the Mentally Ill. He was on Phil Donahue talking about his ordeal and his impressive comeback. As often happens with this tricky disease, the meds stopped helping and he fell off the map yet again. I had occasion to see Lionel again several times in his later years. He was a different person, obviously troubled, a prisoner of his illness.

Despite everything he was going through, the Lionel that I knew then was somewhere still inside. He never forgot my name, always giving a soft-spoken "Hello, Chris" when we saw each other. People often use the phrase, "There, but for the grace of God, go I." Those words are never more poignant than when I think of Lionel's life. He was a sports hero for his exploits on the field, but his heroic nature didn't end there. To me, he remains an even bigger hero for tackling his illness head on like he did so many running backs.

Although he lost the battle in the end, he didn't stop fighting until the final whistle blew. Lionel Aldridge died just a few days shy of his 57th birthday on February 12, 1998. When I think about him now, as I do from time to time, it's with a smile. I think of the Lionel that I got to meet and I pray he is at peace.

By Christopher Peppas

CR SO

96 Sassy & Coach Holmgren

Years ago, while Mike Holmgren was still the Packers coach, I discovered that we kenneled our dogs at the same facility, Golrusk in Green Bay. My long-time wish has been to meet someone from the Packers. Moreover, I had hoped that when the time came, I'd not be so

tongue-tied that I didn't have something to say. One day, I got my opportunity. Unfortunately, things didn't work out quite the way I had hoped, and it was no one's fault but my own.

The day came when I found myself face-to-face with none other than Mike Holmgren. Suddenly, my thoughts scattered. I couldn't think of a thing to say. Everything in me froze up. All I could do was stand there next to him and look up. He was a really big guy!

Meanwhile, my Beagle, Sassy, had no problem making a connection and communicating with him. She walked right over and began to sniff his shoes. I pulled her back a bit, embarrassed by the event, but Mr. Holmgren only noticed Sassy at his feet.

"Hi there, little one," he said with a smile.

She wagged her tail happily in response. I felt like an idiot standing there next to him, unable to make anything come out of my mouth. By now, he had retrieved his own dog, so he left. Naturally, he was no sooner out the door that I got my voice back.

Sassy

I can promise that the next time I get a chance to meet a player or coach I won't be so dog gone quiet!

By Jan Niec

CR SO

97 A Legend's Last Beer City Performance

Packer die-hards will never forget the last game played by the green and gold warriors in Milwaukee's County Stadium December 18, 1994, which was decided by Brett Favre's 9-yard scamper and subsequent lunge over the pylon with only 16-ticks left to score.

Green Bay beat the Atlanta Falcons 21-17. There was another significant date back in 1971 that was similar and the Moerchens were there for it. Ten-year-old John and his father, John Sr., made the one-hour trip from Fond du Lac to witness it.

What John most recalls of the game between the New Orlean Saints and Packers was what his father told him as he watched the rookie Cajun QB scramble for his life.

"Johnny, a kid with guts like that will one day have children to be proud of."

I think it's safe to say that the apple didn't fall too far from the tree for Archie Manning, who has, in fact, produced a couple of good men. Their names? Peyton and Eli. The game that day was between two teams, neither of which was doing terribly well that season. The only difference may have been that even when the Packers aren't doing well, they still manage to fill the stadium.

There's an element of trivia to this game where Packer Quarterbacks are concerned. We'll get to that in a moment. From the '94 clash we recall names like Rich McGeorge, Ken Ellis, Dave Hampton, but on that particular day, the Green Bay quarterback went 8 for 17 for 116 yards, with no touchdowns. He also ran twice for ten yards before giving way to Zeke Bratkowski. Who was he? None other than the great Bart Starr and that was his last game in County Stadium.

To this day, Papa John and son Johnny Moerchen still celebrate the time they spent together at that memorable event, reminding us again that it's not always whether a team wins or loses the game, but what we can learn from those who are playing in it.

Here's a small media summary of the game with stats and box scores from Bart's last game at Milwaukee County Stadium. (I'd guess Charlie Durkee slept pretty well afterward. After all, he was pretty busy that day!)

November 28, 1971: New Orleans Saints (4-5-2) 29, Green Bay Packers (3-7-1) 21

(Milwaukee) - Charlie Durkee kicked five field goals, and rookie Bob Gresham ran for 113 yards. The Saints defense logged two interceptions and four fumble recoveries. Doug Wyatt ended the Packer hopes with a 55-yard interception return in the fourth.

```
NEW ORLEANS -    3   3   6   17  -  29
GREEN BAY -      7   0   0   14  -  21
```

NO	-	Charlie Durkee, 12-yard field goal NEW ORLEANS 3-0
GB	-	Donny Anderson, 3-yard run (Tim Webster kick) GREEN BAY 7-3
NO	-	Charlie Durkee, 12-yard field goal GREEN BAY 7-6
NO	-	Charlie Durkee, 35-yard field goal NEW ORLEANS 9-7
NO	-	Charlie Durkee, 26-yard field goal NEW ORLEANS 12-7
NO	-	Jim Strong, 1-yard run (Charlie Durkee kick) NEW ORLEANS 19-7
GB	-	Dave Hampton, 90-yard kickoff (Tim Webster kick) NEW ORLEANS 19-14
NO	-	Charlie Durkee, 11-yard field goal NEW ORLEANS 22-14
NO	-	Doug Wyatt, 55-yard interception return (Charlie Durkee kick) NO 29-14
GB	-	Rich McGeorge, 40-yard pass from Zeke Bratkowski (Webster kick) NO 29-21

by Steve Rose with memories from John Moerchen

CR SO

98 Walk-in Room Only

On January 12, 1997, the Packers hosted the upstart Carolina Panthers for a return trip to the Super Bowl. Louie Clark, from the small Wisconsin town of Omro, was a college student at Lawrence University in Appleton. Although he couldn't afford tickets to be at the game, he had determined he wasn't going to miss out on the action.

He and his college friends, Matt Kehrein and J.T. Maschman, made the 25-minute drive north to tailgate and watch the game with a family from the Oneida Reservation who had rented a house across the street from Lambeau Field. By the end of the third quarter, it appeared that the Packers were going to be victorious. Louie had an idea.

"Hey, let's go over to the stadium," Louie suggested.

"What for?" asked his friend.

"Let's just go over there to be a part of the action."

Upon their arrival, to their utter disbelief and amazement, they found the doors to Lambeau open! They sauntered right in and stood in the aisles. The entire stadium was on its feet. Louie and company watched the 4th quarter with 50,000 other Packer fans.

After the game, Louie saw a great opportunity. There, on the Jumbotron, was the final score, 30-13. That, however, was not what grabbed his attention and imagination as he captured the Kodak moment for future sharing with his children and grandchildren. The second click of his camera was to capture Reggie White, doing what Reggie White did best, praying on the 50-yard line at Lambeau Field.

That day, Packers fans across the country gave thanks for a victory. How fitting that it was Reggie who reminded us to bow our heads.

In Memoriam to Reggie White, December 19, 1961 – December 26, 2004

By Steve Rose with memories from Louie Clark IV

ભ્ર ૪૦

Reggie White shown on the Jumbotron praying

99 Reggie's Heart

Reggie White was one of the greatest pro football players ever to grace the sod at Lambeau Field. He was an even greater man. Not long after "The Minister of Defense" signed with the Packers because "God told me to," I had the privilege of sitting next to him on the dias at the National Prayer Breakfast in downtown Milwaukee.

Governor Tommy Thompson, a Republican, and John Norquist, the Democratic Milwaukee Mayor at the time, each spoke that day. After observing both, White leaned over and whispered in my ear.

"Those two don't like each other, do they?" he said with a big grin spread across his face.

That was vintage Reggie. He was a bright and intuitive man who loved God with every fiber of his being, and who wasn't afraid to shout it to the mountaintops. Many people scoff at the notion that Reggie White came to Titletown because God told him to come, but I'm not among them.

Christian or not, everyone has the right to be a business man. To think that #92 would pick a smaller market like Green Bay over a larger city such as San Francisco is an indicator that Reggie truly felt led. The emerging Brett Favre at quarterback undoubtedly factored into the equation, as well.

The former Tennessee Volunteer and Philadelphia Eagles star had a vision of the Pack winning the Super Bowl. After it happened, he warned the Packer nation in an interview not to worship the players, but to keep their focus on the God who created them.

I remember a few of White's words to me the night before Super Bowl XXXII against Denver.

"I'm worried about the Broncos," he said quite matter of factly.

Those concerns turned out to be somewhat prophetic.

Reggie told me, smiling from ear to ear, that he treated his beautiful bride Sarah like a queen so that he'd be treated like a king. Reggie and I once talked about me joining him on one of his trips to the Holy Land. I knew how unlikely it would be for that to happen, given how tight our budget was. I joked that it'd take a call directly from him to our General

Manager to get her to even consider the idea.

Shortly after that conversation, the GM brought me into her office and told me about a call she had "on hold." The man was claiming to be Reggie White.

"Sure," she said, not believing for a second that the future Hall of Famer was on the line.

Imagine her shock when she found out it was the Big Dog! I didn't get to go on the trip, but that was a special moment for both of us!

Reggie White's death was a shocking and tragic loss for everyone. From our perspective, he was taken all too soon, but perhaps the Lord just wanted him to "come home" after a job well done. Not everybody believed in what White said, or what he stood for. I remember the flack he took, for example, over his speech to the politicians in Madison.

Whether you agreed with him or not, there's certainly a consensus on one thing. Reggie had a big heart, and his heart was in the right place. It was always in the right place.

By Tom Pipines, WITI Fox6, Milwaukee

CR SO

Reggie White shaking hands with Alyssa McGray

About Steve Rose

Steve burst onto the scene in 1996 with the release of the book *Leap of Faith: God Must Be a Packer Fan*, one of the greatest Packer feel-good books of all time. He is a dynamic and passionate speaker gifted with the ability to help individuals and companies realize their full potential and achieve their purpose. Rose's Peanut Butter Promise seminars and keynotes are in great demand because of the vast personal and professional performance-raising results. Steve lives in Neenah, WI, with his wife Kathi and step-daughter Sarah.

Steve's keynotes and seminars include:
- For Companies & Individuals – 7 Principles of the Peanut Butter Promise
- For Schools – The Power of Purpose for Students
- For Churches – The Parable of 2 Planes

About Kathi Rose

Kathi is an author and eloquent speaker who talks to audiences on a variety of captivating topics. She has survived breast cancer, dealt with the loss of her son and daughter-in-law in a motorcycle accident in 1994 (chronicled in her book *I Climbed a Mountain: A Mother's Diary of Tragedy, Grief & Triumph* released in 1996) and is currently raising a special-needs adult daughter. Kathi is an ordained & licensed minister who is currently serving as co-pastor at Evangel Worship Center in Menasha, WI. She lives with her husband Steve and her daughter Sarah in Neenah, WI.

Kathi's keynotes and seminars include:
- For Companies & Individuals – Spa for the Soul
- For Churches – Chosen, Called & Commissioned
- A variety of teachings available for Women's Retreats

To book Steve and/or Kathi to speak go to:

www.winnerssuccessnetwork.com